Working With Older Adoptees:

A Sourcebook of Innovative Models

Edited by:
Loren Coleman
Karen Tilbor
Helaine Hornby
Carol Boggis

Published in the United States by the University of Southern Maine,
Human Services Development Institute, Portland, Maine 04103

Library of Congress Cataloging in Publication Data

Coleman, Loren; Tilbor, Karen; Hornby, Helaine; and Boggis, Carol, eds.
Working With Older Adoptees

ISBN# 0-939561-05-0
$10.00

1. Adoption. 2. Adoptees—Services. I. Title
Library of Congress 89-199887

Book design and cover by Camille Cole
University of Southern Maine
Office of Publications

Second Printing, 1990.

Copyright Notice/Errata

◐ University of Southern Maine

Table of Contents

Acknowledgements

What is adoption? A child brought into your home? A bigger family? A new brother or sister for an only child? Not so fast! Adoption is not just an event. Adoption is a lifelong process, and this book captures that premise with some groundbreaking contributions for a wide range of professionals presently working with older adoptees. This project would not have been possible without this core of material, and our deep appreciation goes to these contributors.

A book such as this, however, is more than the work of its chapter authors. Many people have supported this effort.

Among the University of Southern Maine's Human Services Development Institute staff, special thanks go to Helaine Hornby and Susan Partridge for the seeds of this project; Carol Sue Hayden, Meg Littlefield, Marie Strnad, and Normajean Forbes for wordprocessing and proofreading; and, of course, my coeditors, Karen Tilbor, Helaine Hornby and Carol Boggis. Funding support for this project comes through Grant Number 90-CO-0286 from the United States Department of Health and Human Services.

In conjunction with this book, we have produced a companion videotape: *Adoption—A Lifelong Process*. The individuals, besides the undersigned, responsible for creating this video are: Karen Tilbor of the University of Southern Maine, Dan Porter of Polar Bear Pictures; Ted Miles, Mara Janelle and Ella Hudson of Expanded Video, Inc.; and David Bean of WGME-TV. They all were extremely important to the process, and added much to the framework of this volume in their overall design of that video. Many of this book's contributors appear in *Adoption—A Lifelong Process*, and our gratitude is extended to them for their assistance in that phase of the project.

In terms of the artistic construction of this book's cover and typesetting, we want to thank Camille Cole and Wendy Wells of the University of Southern Maine Publications for their great work. They were helped in their efforts by Design Access, Type*plus*, and Anne Bernard of the Human Services Development Institute.

Besides the professionals who wrote the chapters, many other individuals interested in working with older adoptees gave us insights and information. These include: Janet Brysh, David Brodzinsky, Mary Jane Fales, Elaine Schwartz, Mary Pat Clemmons, Jane Conner, Susan Klickman, Dawn Degenhardt, Spence Chapin, Post Adoption Services of New York, Lee Campbell, Jon Ryan, Pat Yates, Barbara Bender, Mina Bicknell, Joyce Forsythe, the Walker School, as well as numerous other adoptive parents, older adoptees, birthparents, and adoption professionals. We appreciate their help.

This book reflects the labor of many people willing to share the work they do with older adoptees. We hope you find something useful here for whatever your profession. If you work with children and teens, you are likely to come in contact with someone who has been adopted. (Adoptees, all six million of them in this country, have a definite impact on our social service systems.) Be creative and daring. Remember, every family is unique. And the best kind of treatment for one may not work for the next. Choose an approach that you are comfortable with and discover the types of treatment which are right for you.

The rewards of this work are immense, and the new beginnings for you and these children will be many, since adoption is a lifelong process.

Loren Coleman
August 1988
Portland, Maine

I. Why This Book

The purpose of this book is to present a range of models for providing mental health and other supportive services to older adopted children and their families. In doing so, we review problems experienced by adolescents and pre-adolescents and specific points of intervention during the life of an adopted child or an adoptive family. We distinguish two general types of interventions, clinical and educational-social, and describe selected models for clinical intervention in some detail.

This book is intended for the professional in mental health or child welfare who may be providing services to, or seeking a referral for, the older adopted child and his/her family. The focus is on the pre-adolescent and adolescent-age child. Adoption professionals have identified a growing need for services to children in that age group and their families since the implementation of the Adoption Assistance and Child Welfare Act of 1980, which urged permanency planning for all children and made subsidies available for special needs adoptions. Also, a growing sensitivity to the interrelationship of adoption issues and the developmental stages of childhood, as well as acceptance and publicity surrounding the search process, have heightened public and professional awareness of the need for post-adoption services.

Some issues particular to adoptive families may warrant special consideration in the assessment of a problem and the subsequent recommendation of a response or intervention. While adoptive families may experience difficulties at any point in the adoption process and the life of the family, problems are more likely to surface in the child's adolescent years. Numerous studies of the last 25 years report conflicting conclusions regarding specific differences between adopted and non-adopted peers in both clinical and non-clinical samples. Current experts agree, however, that adoption issues can cause difficulties at various stages of individual and family development and that specific therapeutic interventions and other supportive services, although not always warranted, can help to ease transitions and resolve some problems. While "only a minority of adopted children manifest clinically significant symptomatology...the higher incidence of psychological problems associated with adoption is restricted to children in the middle childhood years and adolescence" (Brodzinsky 1987:29).

In the case of children adopted at older ages, difficulties have been more obviously linked to adoption and to a history that probably included numerous losses, such as leaving birth and foster families, as well as possible abuse and problem behaviors that could not be ignored.

In Judith Schaffer and Ron Kral's article in this volume, they report:

> Adopted children and adolescents, though only an estimated two to four percent of the population, are thought to comprise a disproportionate number of referrals for mental health services.... Families who adopt infants are reported to be somewhat more likely than birthparents to seek professional help for parent/ child difficulties.... Therefore, psychologists, psychiatrists, clinical social workers, mental health counselors, family therapists, nurses and school personnel will have to develop a greater understanding of the needs of adopted individuals and their families, along with an understanding of the normal difficulties associated with this status, in order to effectively understand and help them.
>
> Treating the adoptive family requires sensitivity to more than the psychology of an individual adoptee. It requires educating parents about the normal course of child development along with the unique developmental tasks of the adopted child. It may also necessitate actively convincing adoptive parents that they possess the necessary skills, attitudes and abilities to raise adopted children successfully.

In the past, services provided to adoptive families by adoption agencies continued from the time of placement until the adoption was finalized. Following legalization of adoption services, agency ties were terminated and families in need of specialized services, including mental health services, obtained them within their own communities if resources were available. If therapy was required, issues relating to the adoptive status of the individual may have been unrecognized or ignored as irrelevant, especially if the adoption occurred years before.

Increased acceptance of the adoptee's option to search for birthparents and siblings (or the birthparent's option to search for a biological child), and the influence of adoption issues on the adolescent's search for identity, have created a demand for post-adoption services that did not exist before. Some agencies have initiated services, sometimes in separate post-adoption departments, ranging from assisting with search inquiries to offering clinical services for children with serious behavior problems.

It became apparent to some agency professionals that the success of many older child adoptions depended in part on providing a range of services to these families and continuing them indefinitely. According to Fales in the Child Welfare League of America study of post-adoption services (1986: 9), agency programs were based on the following concepts:

1. Adoption is a different and complex way of creating a family that may then encounter unique problems based on the adoptive status.

2. Open communication within the family about adoption and the differences it can make is desirable.

3. Unresolved feelings of the parents about infertility must be dealt with.

4. Post-legal adoption services should be identified as part of an agency's adoption service from the onset of the process, and more honest communication encouraged at every step of the way.

5. Post-legal adoption needs of families should be handled by professionals who understand and are sensitive to the differences between biological and adoptive issues in parenting.

Not all adoption agencies have the resources to develop post-legal adoption programs, but their doing so is not the only route to expanding services to families after finalization. Adoption agencies can play a key role in informing existing mental health providers of the needs of the adoption population and thereby contributing to the expansion of services in their respective states. Existing models represent several approaches to providing post-adoption services. There is no unanimity about the best therapeutic model. The field is not limited to a particular approach, but in a defined geographical area there may be only a single service available or none. Adoption professionals agree that in general, available services are insufficient and not always geographically well-distributed; information about programs is often inaccessible to families in need. An adoptive family ought to be able to choose the service that best meets its needs, given adequate information and the resources to follow through.

Traditionally, the relationship between the mental health and child welfare professions has been characterized by limited interaction and little mutual knowledge or awareness. The growing demand for mental health services to older adopted children and their families has highlighted the importance of developing a closer collaboration between mental health and child welfare. There is a need to expand the number of qualified mental health practitioners who know the special issues which may affect adoptees and their families and can integrate them into their treatment approaches. Similarly, child welfare professionals need to know the treatment options available in order to consider what services the agency itself might provide, and to be able to make appropriate referrals with confidence that adoptive families will be well-served.

To offer a sample of models that address this need, we collected works by nationally-recognized practitioners who offer creative solutions for treating older adoptees and their families. These authors richly illustrate their topics with case studies.

Section II looks at family issues that are causes for intervention, and the roles that child development stages and crises play in the evolution of healthy adoptions.

Section III delves into clinical intervention models in greater detail. These are selected for their usefulness and innovativeness as clinical interventions with older adoptees. The authors discuss such topics as pre-intervention preparation; the need for specialized post-adoption services and methods of child and parent evaluation; teen and parent group therapy approaches; brief, targeted therapies; mentor modeling; and ways to maximize benefits from crisis intervention.

The book, in Section IV, gives a brief presentation of ideas for educational and social interventions, and examines the search as a ovement and a resource.

Short biographical information on the book's editors and authors is found in Section V.

Bibliographical information is presented for the entire volume's collection of works at the conclusion of the book.

II. Points of Intervention

In this section, Kenneth W. Watson of Chicago Child Care Society and Jean-Pierre Bourguignon of Illinois' Consultants in Developmental Behavioral Dysfunction identify seven areas of difficulty that cause barriers to successful adoptions. These include problems with developing feelings of entitlement and claiming the child emotionally; unmatched expectations of parents and adoptees; shifting family systems due to new members; separation, loss and grief issues; bonding and attachment problems; and effects of adoption on identity formation. The authors provide insights into these issues and their causes, and suggest ways the professional can help family members work through them. The material is developed from their original discussion of this topic in *After Adoption* (Bourguignon and Watson, 1987).

Also, Karen Tilbor of the University of Southern Maine discusses the roles that child development stages and crises play in adoptive situations. A developmental approach offers an alternative view of crises in an adoptee's life.

Areas of Difficulty in Adoptions
Kenneth W. Watson
Jean-Pierre Bourguignon

The difficulties experienced by adoptive families usually fall into one of seven related areas. Familiarity with these areas and ideas about suitable responses can help the professional work more constructively with adoptive families.

1. Entitlement

Entitlement means the adoptive parents sense that they have the *right* to be parents to their child. It is essential to the parent-child bond.

Entitlement comes in two forms: legal and emotional. The legal right is granted with the adoption decree. The emotional right comes more slowly, and must be carefully nurtured. Until this right develops the adoptive parents may hold back in their commitment and responses to the child, with predictable consequences — especially regarding discipline.

External factors may inhibit a sense of entitlement. Perhaps, by plan, members of the child's biological family remain active in the child's life, and adoptive parents may feel they share the child with them. An agency may still be active in the relationship, again fostering the sense that parenthood is being shared. Members of the extended adoptive family may have reservations about the wisdom of adoption, or of adopting this particular child.

Community attitudes may transmit the message to adoptive parents that they do not have full claim to the child. When a couple becomes biological parents, for example, the arrival of the new child is often greeted with showers of gifts. Adoptive parents rarely experience this response. Biological parents are often eligible for maternity leave from their jobs; adoptive parents rarely are. In addition, parenthood training classes and support groups for new parents tend to be directed toward biological parents.

Internal factors may add to the problem. Adoptive parents may feel residual ambivalence about the wisdom of the adoption decision. There may also be lingering, unresolved feelings about the parents' infertility. Adoptive parents may harbor some guilt about taking the child from the biological parents, or fear that the biological parents (or the adoption agency) might someday return and reclaim the child. Another fear adoptive parents may have is that, at some point, their adopted children will search for and find their birthparents, and will relinquish their ties to the adopted family.

One can encourage the development of emotional entitlement by finding opportunities to sanction and support the adoption while recognizing the ambivalence the parents may feel. The professional might help by putting adoptive parents in touch with appropriate support groups, or by serving as an advocate for adoptive parents in difficult situations, for example, situations where the parental rights of adoptive parents have been called into question (such as when the parents apply for special schooling or remedial services that the child might need).

2. Claiming

Claiming is the process by which the adoptive parents come to accept an adopted child as their own, and as a full-fledged member of the family. Claiming begins with the adoptive parents' capacity to find and identify similarities between the child and themselves (or other family members), rather than focusing only on the differences.

While the differences that adoption makes for a child should not be denied, the adopted child is entitled to the same kind of acceptance and status within the family as are the biological children. The similiarities between two such children are far greater than any differences.

If the professional is involved with an adoptive family at the time of adoption, some steps can be suggested that may facilitate the claiming process. If the child is an unnamed infant, it might be suggested to the family that they consider giving the child a family name or a name that ties the child to the family's history in some way. If the child is already named, a nickname or a new middle name might be selected. This procedure works well with older children, since it can be applied at any time in a child's life.

Parents can also share family picture albums with the older adopted child. They can encourage members of the extended family to write to the child, enclosing family pictures and requesting snapshots of the child. Pictures of the adopted child should be included in the family album. Pictures of the adoptive family, with the new member, should also be included in the album immediately and circulated among members of the extended family.

Many older children coming into adoption will bring a Life Book with them. This is a scrapbook containing pictures, photos and comments about the child's life up to this placement.

A Life Book, if started before placement in an adoptive family, may be a therapeutic tool to help the child deal with the painful events of the past. If continued into adoption, the book may serve a number of useful purposes, one of which is the furtherance of the claiming process. As the child and adoptive parents periodically review the book together and add materials that bring it up to date, the child can be helped to see that the adoption did not erase the past, nor create a new person. One's early history and former identities do remain, and must be integrated into the present. The parents can help the child accomplish this, and can further the claiming process by pointing out similarities between the past and present.

The new child must be told about family history, traditions and rituals and included in them. By the same token, the adoptive family should learn from the child about rituals and traditions from the child's former families. These should be incorporated into the life of the current family.

New rituals should also be created to include the adopted child. A celebration of the day on which the child entered the family, or the day on which the adoption was consummated, might serve this purpose. Additional family rituals unrelated to the adoption help children feel that their ties to the family do not depend wholly on their adopted status.

3. Unmatched Expectations

Unmatched expectations mean that although both the adopted children and the families adopting them enter into their new relationship with high expectations, these expectations have very little in common.

The situation of unmatched expectations causes more difficulties for adoptive families than anything else — especially in the early stages of adoption. Both parents and child feel they have made an emotional investment in the adoption — an investment that may involve considerable stress — and each looks forward to some return on the investment.

If individual expectations of each party were clear, and if both parties were aware that the other had different — but equally important — expectations, it would be theoretically possible to negotiate mutually acceptable agenda. However, individual agenda are often deeply rooted in the emotional histories of parent and child, and are not easily changed. Even when change occurs, abandoning the original expectation represents yet another loss.

Nevertheless, it is important for some common ground to be reached; otherwise, the new family is in serious jeopardy. A professional's task can be to help the family recognize these unmatched expectations, mourn those that can never be, and search together for other, alternative satisfactions or a compromise.

4. Shifting Family Systems

Shifting family systems means that when an adopted child enters a family, the family balance is changed. Each family member must then adjust to these changes, and to a corresponding shift in expectations.

With shifting of family systems comes a change in patterns of everyday family life. For example, formal or informal rules for getting up in the morning, or taking turns in the bathroom, must be altered to accommodate the new member. In fact, most of the rules of family living, arrived at after months or years of adjustment, must suddenly be altered.

When an infant is born to the family, he or she arrives after a planning period of several months. The child arrives in a helpless state, making concessions from other family members necessary. This chain of events does not hold for an adopted child, particularly an older child.

With the arrival of an adopted child, the adult members of the household may understand, at least intellectually, the need to accommodate the new person. Nevertheless, altering family patterns graciously does not happen easily or overnight. For the other children in the household, the task of accommodation will be more difficult. The arrival of a newly adopted child will create resentment on the part of the birth children, and will threaten the security of other adopted children — awakening in them earlier questions or trauma from their own origins or history.

10

At points of family stress, an adoption may play a crucial role in the generation or resolution of conflict. In any ordinary family system, children have a way of dividing parents. An adopted child, as an "outsider," is much more likely to play this role, and may become the symptom bearer for the family system.

If infertility is an issue, the adopted child will be an ever-present reminder of that infertility. If infertility is a point of contention between the parents, the adopted child is likely to receive the fallout. Generally, in most two-parent adoptive families, one parent was more enthusiastic for adoption than the other, and that parent finds it easier to establish claiming ties to the child. The child thus becomes, in yet another way, a focal point for divisiveness.

Another problem that may arise is the adopted child's resistance at attempts to incorporate him or her into the family system. Older children, even if well prepared for an adoption and hopeful that it will work out, will come into the new home with a history of living in family systems that did not work. They will perceive the new family in the light of past experience, and any initial responses are likely to be ones learned in the past. Consciously or unconsciously, these children may be looking for weaknesses to exploit in order to validate their past experiences.

Attention to these problems prior to the adoption placement, and during the period immediately following placement, may help the family to deal constructively with these difficulties. It is important, however, that the adoptive family recognizes and accepts that a family never adopts just a child — but rather a *whole new extended family system.*

Techniques for mapping past and current family structures, such as famographs, genograms (Hartman 1979) and ecomaps (Hartman 1978), can help adoptive families and professionals better understand family systems created by adoption.

Professionals can help the adoptive family develop an awareness of the ways in which their family works. Helpful suggestions may include creating a family discussion time exclusively for working together on family issues, or making the continuation of the adopted child's Life Book a family project.

5. Separation, Loss and Grief

Loss is the affectual state one experiences when something of significance is unexpectedly withdrawn. Separation, whether temporary or permanent, from meaningful relationships precipitates an acute sense of loss. Grief is the process through which one passes in order to recover from a loss.

Loss is a universal human experience, and a pervasive area of concern in adoptive situations. Adopting adults must deal with the "loss" of the biological child they did not have; the adopted child must deal with the loss of the birth family, and possibly siblings or other meaningful foster family members. Both must deal with the loss of control over their lives inherent in any involvement with an adoption agency and the legal system.

Painful as these losses may be, they may serve a useful purpose for adoptive families. Sharing losses allows parent and child to touch each other at a meaningful level, when they may have little else in common.

Although helping with loss may not be the most appropriate point to initiate therapeutic intervention with a given adoptive family, one must not lose sight of the fact that it is a dominant aspect of the family's situation. Loss is always the "stage set" before which the current adoption drama is played out.

To understand these families, the professional needs to have a model of the stages of grief in mind. Several models exist, such as those of J. Perlmutter (1972), E. Kubler-Ross (1969) and B. Simos (1979). In the real world, of course, the stages in the grief process may not occur in the same order as in the conceptual model.

In helping the family deal with grief, it is important to realize that grief is never fully resolved, and that each new loss will bring forth unresolved feelings dating from earlier losses. Grief can only be worked through in a context of stability, and it is worked through most successfully with someone else's help.

6. Bonding and Attachment

Bonding refers to the unique tie between child and biological parent, primarily the mother. Children truly bond only to their birthparents.

Attachment is the psychologically rooted tie between two people that permits them to have affectual significance for each other.

Bonding begins with the onset of pregnancy (or the decision to become a parent), and develops through a complex physiological and psychological process before, during and immediately after birth. Because of its pre-natal, biologic origins, *this primal bonding persists regardless of later separations.*

The ability to form attachments is acquired as a child moves through the developmental stages of the first three years of life. At birth, a child is physically and psychologically dependent upon adults. As children learn to distinguish self from environment and to recognize persons who are essential to their well-being, they learn to tolerate separation from the caregiving adult. This is achieved only when the child believes that this adult will again return.

Poor parenting may result in a child failing to learn how to make meaningful attachments. In addition, even if this ability is learned, it can subsequently be damaged by poor or interrupted parenting. Either situation can result in what is known as "attachment disorder."

Serious attachment disorders may require clinical attention. However, adoptive parents can be supported in nurturing attachments with their adopted children. While it is never possible to go back and make up for developmental short-changes, it is possible to identify the areas in which a child was short-changed and respond sensitively to those needs. Parental consistency, coupled with a willingness to allow the child to regress and seek the nurturing that was unavailable at an earlier developmental level, can be helpful.

7. Identity Formation

Identity is the sense that one is a "self" — and that the self has identifiable boundaries and value.

A sense of personal identity is formed, both consciously and unconsciously, through experiences, interaction with and exposure to other people, and by making decisions concerning who and what one will be. Identity is rooted in the family history, nurtured through the natural processes of development, and shaped by individual and family dynamics.

While one's identity is never fully formed, much of the developmental work occurs when a child is three or four, and again in adolescence. Children of kindergarten age know the family to whom they belong, and know something about the boundaries between that family and the outside world. Children at this stage have also learned about sexual characteristics. During adolescence, the child learns to deal with new sexual feelings and with the prospect of leaving the family upon reaching maturity.

Adopted children face unique difficulties in identity formation. The foremost difficulty is the damage to their self-image stemming from the fact that their biological parents "gave them away." An adopted child may also be working from distorted factual information about personal and family history, or may be missing critical pieces of information—such as a mother's or father's name, ancestry, or ethnic heritage. If a child's earlier developmental tasks have not been successfully completed, confusion regarding sexual or family identity may result.

Formation of sexual identity may be especially complicated for adopted children since their choice of parental role models is ambiguous. They may identify with their biological parents, who were able to have children but not to rear them, or with their adoptive parents, who were able to rear children but not to have them.

The professional can support the adopted child struggling to form identity by helping to build self-esteem. Accurate information about a child's origins or history will provide a more solid base. In this context, again, a Life Book can be a useful tool.

Occasionally, in an attempt to be *someone,* an adopted child will focus prematurely on an identity and become fixed in it. Sometimes that early identity works out, but often it limits the child, and allows for only the narrowest self-definition.

For example, some children may seize too tightly on their adopted status, never allowing themselves the opportunity to be more than an 'adopted person,' and thwarting any opportunity to develop their potential as a fully integrated being. Attempts should be made to keep the child's identity boundaries flexible until well into adolescence.

The issues of loss, self-worth, and identity converge at the point of an adopted person's interest in information about, and search for, the birthparents. Part of the reason for this search is the wish to see someone who is blood kin, and whom one may look like or be like. Another part is the wish to ask this person, "Why did you give me up?"

8. Points to Remember: An Overview and Summary

Adoptive families most often experience difficulties in seven areas:

- Entitlement
- Claiming

- Unmatched expectations
- Shifting family systems
- Separation, loss and grief
- Bonding and attachment
- Identity formation

In particular, understanding the following points aids in helping adoptive families:

- Infertility is frequently a critical issue in adoptive families.
- The Life Book is often a useful tool, both before and after an adoption.
- Shared family rituals will help solidify the adopted child's position in the family.
- The initial expectations of adoptive parents and the adopted child never match.
- Family systems tend initially to reject new members.
- When one adopts a child, one adopts a whole new extended family system.
- A sense of loss may serve as a point of emotional contact between adoptive parents and adopted child.
- Grief is never resolved.
- Grief can only be worked out in a context of stability.
- Grief is best worked out with another person, not alone.
- A sense of identity includes a sense of self, of boundaries and of self-worth.

Influence of Developmental Stages and Crises
Karen Tilbor

Understanding the potential impact of adoption issues at various stages of child development can help the adoptive family prepare for difficulties should they occur. Adoption agency professionals, school professionals, mental health and medical professionals are among those who can play a role in educating and supporting parents as they respond to their child's needs at various stages — needs whose symptoms may be as basic as a direct question about adoption or as puzzling and disturbing as behavior change which occurs for no apparent reason. Knowledge of the interrelationship between adoption issues and normal development is relevant whether the child was adopted as an infant or as a teenager.

A reconceptualization of post-placement services in this revolution in adoption requires that post-adoption services be available on an as-needed basis throughout the growing-up period of the child.

At various key times throughout the developmental cycle of the child and of the family the issue of adoption emerges and puts special demands on both child and family. For example, emerging concerns about identity and identity formation during a child's adolescent years frequently reawaken interest in biological roots and child and family may well need help in dealing with this. The search movement has underlined the specialness of the adoptive status and the fact that, for many, the connection of the biological family is never totally severed even for an adoptee who has been relinquished and adopted in the early weeks of life (Hartman 1984:3).

Table 1. A Psychosocial Model of Adoption Adjustment[1]

Age Period	Erikson's Psychosocial Crises[2]	Adoptive Family Tasks
Infancy	Trust vs. mistrust	Resolving feelings regarding infertility Coping with uncertainty and anxiety related to the placement process Finding appropriate role models and developing realistic expectations regarding adoptive parenthood Coping with the social stigma surrounding adoption Developing secure attachment relationships in cases of delayed placement
Toddlerhood & Preschool Years	Autonomy vs. shame & doubt Initiative vs. guilt	Coping with the anxiety and uncertainty surrounding the initial telling process Creating an atmosphere in which questions about adoption can be freely explored
Middle Childhood	Industry vs. inferiority	Helping the child master the meaning of adoption Helping the child in the initial stages of adaptive grieving Maintaining an atmosphere in which questions about adoption can be freely explored in light of the complications brought about by the grief process
Adolescence	Ego identity vs. identity confusion	Helping the adolescent cope with genealogical bewilderment Helping the adolescent grieve for the lost self (in addition to the loss of birthparents and origins) Maintaining an atmosphere in which questions about adoption can be freely explored in light of the complications associated with the grief process (including support for the adolescent's/young adult's search for origins)

[1]Brodzinsky (1987:31)
[2]Erikson (1968)

Depending upon the age of the child at the time of adoption and the initiation of mental health services, accepting a developmental approach to dealing with adoption issues offers the potential for preventing or reducing the severity of later difficulties. Table 1, developed by Dr. David Brodzinsky, illustrates the correspondence between Erikson's psychosocial crises and the adoption-related tasks the child and family must accomplish during the stages of infancy, toddlerhood/preschool years, school age years, and adolescence. Brodzinsky, in research treating adopted children, provides staunch support for a developmental perspective regarding adoption. Addressing the development of "basic trust," he suggests that children adopted within approximately the first six months of life develop secure attachment relationships with their mothers, in contrast to those placed beyond the first year for whom complications are more likely to develop. Brodzinsky notes such complications occur, according to Bowlby, "either because of acute distress accompanying the severing of a previously established attachment relationship, or because the child has never developed a secure attachment...as a result of multiple foster placements" (Brodzinsky 1987:32). Depending upon the circumstances, the risks are enhanced for children adopted at progressively older ages.

Related to psychosocial crises, it is often during a crisis that a family will seek post-adoption counseling and be most open to working towards change. Some models of post-adoption counseling focus on the crisis, while others use the crisis situation as an opportunity to help the child and the family understand and resolve past issues. Frequently, the two approaches are combined. [Crisis issues are addressed more fully in this book's chapter by Lauren Frey.]

As the child's understanding of the significance of his/her adoption deepens during the school years, behavioral changes that cause concern to parents and teachers are likely to be the result of the normal process of adaptive grieving (Brodzinsky 1987:36). The following excerpt details the progression of adaptive grieving into adolescence and its bearing on the search for identity.

> Adopted adolescents are often at a disadvantage in their struggle to develop a secure identity. Lacking knowledge about their origins, including who their birthparents are, and why they were relinquished,

adopted adolescents often find it more difficult to form a complete and stable sense of self. They sometimes experience what Sants has called "genealogical bewilderment"—confusion, uncertainty, and a sense of incompleteness regarding their origins. These feelings are an extension of the normal process of adaptive grieving discussed earlier. However, adolescents not only grieve the loss of the unknown birthparents—which is found among elementary school age children as well—but they also grieve the loss of part of themselves. Thus, in adolescence the process of grief and bereavement becomes more complex and certainly more abstract (Brodzinsky 1987:37).

A developmental understanding of adoption can provide a basis for handling predictable issues in the family life of the child adopted as an infant. The benefits in the case of older child adoption may be less obvious. To the extent that problems experienced by children adopted at older ages are the result of occurrences in their early life, parents may be better able to understand and respond to the child's age-inappropriate needs and behavior if they are aware of developmental issues.

The "regression to previous developmental levels is the mechanism which allows the child to seek the nurturing that was missed in earlier years. The reliving of these earlier stages makes it possible for the child to complete his entrance into the new family system" (Gill 1978:273).

In summary, a developmental approach to adoption and to the provision of post-adoption services accepts that adoption is a lifelong issue that imposes specific challenges on the normal developmental process. Families and professionals who are aware of those challenges will be better able to handle difficulties and determine when outside support is warranted.

III. Innovative Clinical Models of Intervention

Increasing interest in the adoptee's search for biological parents and the need to provide support for adoptees and birthparents, as well as the greater availability of special-needs children for adoption, have served as catalysts for the development of post-adoption services. Agencies responsible for recruiting families and placing special-needs children have recognized that the successful continuation of many adoptions depends on early initiation and ongoing provision of services. Such services may reduce difficulties and increase the likelihood that families will seek help when problems do occur. A range of available post-adoption services can reduce the risk of disruption and enhance the growth of adoptive family relationships.

The following factors, identified by Partridge, Hornby, and McDonald (1986:15-16), help us recognize situations which warrant post-adoption services:

> *Mismatch:* The presence of negative characteristics in a child that the parents cannot tolerate; the absence of positive, highly valued characteristics that the parents desire; incompatible personalities or life-styles.

> *Inadequate preparation:* Placement of a child who has not minimally resolved past losses and future expectations; acceptance of a child by a family that does not possess the knowledge about adoption or skills adequate to handle a special needs child.

> *Lack of family supports and resources:* Absence of concrete, emotional help from friends and relatives or presence of negative influence from them; inability of family to seek out and use community support.

> *Lack of empathy and incomplete attachments:* The parents'

inability to interpret the meaning of the child's behavior; the child's inability to recognize the parents' sincere level of concern; the sense of disappointment that builds when emotional bonds do not form.

Family system strain and overload: The peak of stress when numerous factors, internal and external, collectively impinge on the family, making it unable to survive the crisis.

Insurmountable obstacles: The continuation of extreme difficulties that are present early in a high-risk placement.

These authors go on to say (pp. 39-40) that:

Whether or not the adoption agency can provide a range of post-adoption services, it is recommended that the agency:

1. Evaluate the appropriateness of the services which are offered to children and to parents or to which referrals are made.

2. Explore new or additional resources in an effort to expand the range and variety of services. In some cases, it is important to locate appropriate services that the family can afford.

3. Stay involved as a supportive and caring party, encouraging active use of resources.

4. Advocate for appropriate and adequate provision of services, such as from special education programs, medical care facilities, mental health care, recreational or other programs.

5. Nurture a sense of teamwork with parents and with children, particularly with parents who view the agency as an authority figure. Parents who see themselves as equal partners, as equal resources, and children who feel a sense of involvement in making things work will be most likely to communicate problems at a point when something can still be done.

6. Advocate for greater community awareness of special

needs adoptions, to help raise the consciousness of service providers to the needs and situations of adoptive families.

7. Trust your judgments. Early concerns can become later disasters. It's better not to ignore problems for fear of disruption than to confront and work on them.

To introduce the subject of clinical intervention, Kenneth W. Watson and Jean-Pierre Bourguignon concisely list tasks the therapist should perform to prepare for such an intervention.

Foster Cline explains why specialized post-adoption services are needed; points out issues to be aware of in evaluating the family and adopted child; probes variables contributed by the therapist; and makes generalizations and recommendations for treatment techniques, illustrated by case studies.

Joan McNamara's Family Resources staff takes a team approach to special-needs adoption services, to provide a supportive framework for adoptive families. Family and group therapies are integral parts of this comprehensive adoption program, whose components include parenting preparation, Buddy Families and social activities along with placement services.

Deborah Silverstein and Sharon Kaplan discuss seven lifelong issues triggered by the adoption process in birth and adoptive families and their adoptees. These include loss, rejection, guilt and shame, grief, identity, intimacy, and mastery and control, reflecting some of the same concerns discussed in Section II by Watson and Bourguignon. Recognizing and airing these problems can help families to alleviate them.

Judith Schaffer and Ron Kral describe the dimensions of the need for psychiatric services for adoptive families. They have utilized brief, solution-focused therapy with 180 such families, in which they attempt to target and eliminate specific faulty interactions and habits by tapping the potential of family members. Case studies illustrate, and the therapy format is detailed.

Claudia Jewett is interviewed here to provide a personal insight into her therapy methods as used in work with older adoptees. Her successes are offered as models for other therapists, who can apply her techniques to their own cases.

Section III concludes with explorations of crisis intervention. Post-adoption counseling described by Lauren Frey employs a four-week intervention model for older special-needs children.

Crises are viewed as valuable points of entry for problem-solving. Frey relates creative ways of dealing with specific cases.

Foster Cline uses intrusive, confrontational therapies for dealing with some cases. These preclude the need for trust of the therapist by the client, and can include holding therapy, rage reduction therapy, purposeful containment, intrusive high confrontation, time-limited scoldings, physical methods, and outdoor awareness programs. Indications for use, and the process that intrusive techniques follow, are described and a case illustrates the use of holding therapy.

Before Beginning the Intervention

Kenneth W. Watson
Jean-Pierre Bourguignon

Adoptive families, particularly those who have adopted children with special needs, are not conventional families, and many conventional therapies, such as non-directive counseling, behavior management, and individual play therapy may meet with limited success.

Adoptive families need immediate relief. They need *validation* of themselves as parents, and they need *validation* of their adoption plan. Adoptive families must feel that their therapist understands them and is prepared to give them concrete, helpful information and advice.

Therefore, to address the family's issues effectively, the therapist needs to accomplish the following:

- Review the previous assessment; have a solid understanding of the parents' expectations of the child before the adoption as well as their current expectations.

- Arrange the issues uncovered by the assessment in order of priority.

- Set practical short-term and long-term goals.

- Design strategies of intervention to meet those goals.

- Establish a working alliance with the parents.

Adoptive parents are often painfully aware of the gulf that separates them from their adopted child. When working with adoptive families, the professional must be willing to work closely with the parents, and to include them in all aspects of the therapeutic work.

Included in the work with the family should be a provision under which either the family or counselor may withdraw and terminate the working relationship. This will provide a mechanism for ending the process in the event that neither family nor child is experiencing relief.

Post-Placement Services for Adoptive Families — An Overview
Foster Cline

1. The Need for Specialized Services

Good therapists are a dime a dozen. They're everywhere. Yet, good services for adopted children are lacking. Adoptive parents have a hard time finding adequate help. Why is this? Because adopted children have their own set of very special needs. Adopted children and their families do require therapists who specialize in this area, and there aren't many. Unfortunately, many fine individual and family therapists may not be helpful or, may even be somewhat destructive to families working through post-adoptive issues.

In addition to the usual individual and family dynamics present in all families, post-adoptive families are dealing with numerous special situations:

a. Adopted children may arrive in the family with a great deal of psychological baggage that includes grief from the loss of previous families, anger about previous rejection, poor self-image occasioned by previous moves, and distance from intimate relationships. These may lead the child to resist the adoption itself.

b. Many times older adopted children have suffered neglect and abuse as infants or toddlers, leading to thought disorders and psychological problems. The thought disorder usually shows up as problems with causal thinking. For instance, a child may deny taking food when the food was put there for the child. Or the child may be seen hitting another child and then deny having done it. In addition to these disorders in thought, the child may have problems with basic trust (first year of adoption), autonomy (second year), or industry and initiative (third year). Children who lack trust will not bond to their caretakers. Children who have autonomy problems are difficult to control and generally angrily resistant. Children who have initiative and industry problems often "simply quit." As one mother noted, "John is like one of these little cars with a fly wheel that you rub four times vigorously along the ground and then put it down and the car generally goes like hell. However, John has no fly wheel!"

c. Genetics may play a great role in family dynamics. Birth children fit the family genetically. Adopted children may not. Activity level, talents, proclivity for special problems, reactions under stress and many other personality characteristics are present on a genetic basis. Twin studies of children adopted at birth into different families increasingly are showing the power of genetics. Although all children need to be loved and accepted for being themselves, this is particularly true and sometimes particularly difficult in adoptive families. Siblings to the adopted child may feel the child is definitely different: "I don't know — I know she's not like the rest of us are!" as one eight-year-old boy described his adopted sister.

d. If children have been physically or sexually abused in previous families, they show the effects strongly. For instance, sexually abused children often become "sexualized" and confuse sexuality and love. They may be very provocative with other children, while at the same time being very frightened by sex. One mother noted, "If there are two dragonflies mating within 500 yards, Imogene knows about it!" Another adoptive mother noted to a neighbor lady, "I am worried about the kids playing house. However, my child plays house different than your child plays house!"

e. Adoptive parents who must sometimes be more structured or disciplinary with their adopted child run the risk of being misunderstood by relatives and friends. Parents trying to structure the time and activities of children who may fragment easily are seen as over-controlling by uninformed others.

f. When adopting an older child, parents may unwittingly place their marital relationship at risk. There are a number of reasons. First, children who have been placed in many different homes are often angry at mothering figures. Children may be very sneaky with the anger they show the mother, and the father simply sees his wife as overreacting. Second, many sexualized children are winsome, manipulative and provocative in a way that the father does not see but the mother easily notices. Third, if one parent wanted to adopt more than the other, the couple relationship is stressed with recriminations, guilt and justification.

g. Children who have attachment and bonding problems, and there are many in the older adopted group, are friendly and winsome to strangers while distant, unresponsive and unloving to their loving parents. When there are severe problems between parents and children, outsiders often see it as the parents' fault. It is particularly difficult for family, neighbors and friends to believe how difficult a child can be for the parents when the child is so obviously loving to relative strangers.

In summary, it is all too simple for the run-of-the-mill family or individual therapist not to take the special needs of the adoptive family into account. They are liable to see the plea of a birthsibling, "Can we please unadopt!" as a problem with the birthchild rather than a possible symptom of lack of attachment of the adopted child. The experience of one clinical psychologist when visiting an adoptive family is typical. He stated, "Before I really got to know this family, I didn't really realize how one child could terrify a group of others. And I thought that kid was being scapegoated!"

2. Assessment of the Family

Many post-adoptive families have problems. These vary from disruption (the child separates permanently from the family) to mild "usual" family disagreements. When families are in conflict, it is especially important to figure out how much is the child's problem, how much is the parents' problem, how much is a combination, how much is "usual family dynamics," and finally, how much is "adopted family dynamics."

a. Evaluating the Adopted Child

The history of the adopted child is extremely important. Is there a possibility of fetal alcohol syndrome? Were birth and delivery normal? Was the child wanted? What was the early infant/mother relationship? Was the child cuddly? Were there feeding disorders? Was there colic? Were there early hospitalizations, moves from home to home or pain the parents could not relieve? What were the milestones? When did the child walk, speak in sentences, crawl, show a reciprocal smile, parallel play and interactive play? Early school history is very important. How did the child behave in pre-school and kindergarten?

During the first sixteen months of life, the brain is developing. Any child who has a grave break in his or her relationship with the primary caretaker, who suffers pain that the parent cannot remove, or who is subjected to abuse or neglect, runs the risk of having attachment or bonding problems. Although such problems are not inevitably present, it does not surprise us when they are.

The child's school history is very important. If the child is not a problem during pre-school or kindergarten, if he or she did not have problems with the other children or did not act out problems with the teacher, he or she does *not* have attachment and bonding problems. In Evergreen we have found that children who did well with their parents through age 3 can be reached easily with the usual therapeutic techniques. On the other hand, children with attachment and bonding problems who experience difficulties during the first two years of life and show these problems thereafter need very specialized techniques, often involving therapeutic holding and, sometimes, severe confrontation.

In summary, children who have a very real and difficult problem may appear to be made "scapegoats" by the family and other children within the family. Understanding early history, school behavior and developmental milestones often helps us sort out which party really has the problem.

b. Evaluation of the Adoptive Family

Which parent wanted to adopt? Which parent had the happiest childhood? Which parent gets along with his or her own parents and in-laws now? What can the parent's brothers and sisters tell us about their sibling's childhood? If the parents are young, what do their high school records show? What kinds of academic grades and citizenship marks did they receive? How were the parents perceived by their own aunts and uncles? How strong is the marriage? When the parents fill out a questionnaire *independently*, is there congruence? Do both agree on the following?

- Strengths of the marriage.
- Adjectives that describe themselves.
- Adjectives that describe their spouse.
- Issues most likely to disrupt the marriage.
- Primary messages from one to the other.

It is important to identify the strengths and weaknesses that were present in family functioning, including the birthchildren, before the adoption took place. This information about the parental functioning and functioning of the birthchildren helps us clinically to decide if we want to focus on family interaction patterns or the behavior of the adopted child, on helping parents with parenting techniques or working with the child in re-parenting techniques.

3. Therapist Variables

A therapist need not experience marriage to be a good marriage counselor, but it definitely helps. A therapist need not ever have been a parent to adequately teach and work therapeutically with parents, but it helps. Similarly, a therapist need not ever have had foster children or adoptive children in the home to work adequately with foster and adoptive parents — but, again, it helps.

These statements contrast with the old medical adage, "You don't have to have your own gall bladder out to take out a gall bladder!" However true this may be, a physician's *feelings* about his own gall bladder do not affect how he operates on another. However, our feelings do affect our therapy. In fact, there are some schools of thought that feel therapists *primarily* use their own feelings and gut reactions as a guide in therapeutic intervention. I disagree. In disagreement, I feel reasoned thought is essential to objective and professional treatment.

Thought is needed to counteract the influence of a therapist's own background. After fifteen years of clinical supervision of therapists, I have no doubt that the therapist's own life experience definitely affects clinical interventions. For instance, many counselors who were themselves abused as children gravitate to the field of child abuse and unconsciously identify strongly with the child and blame parents. Therapists who have worked things out within their own marriages are more likely to encourage their clients to work things out within the marriage — even when the marriage should be ended! Therapists who have wandered through a number of different marriages tend to guide a couple toward dissolution even when the marriage could work.

It is essential for the therapist to be firmly grounded in normal child development and psychodynamics. If the therapist does not know the age at which normal children can make a circle, square and diamond, the therapist will be at a loss when trying to evaluate both regression and improvement.

The best therapists have a wide range of therapeutic tricks and methods. They are good at couple therapy, family therapy and individual methods. However, of all the therapist's traits, none are more important than an honest, non-judgmental empathic approach.

These traits result in the therapist conveying to the adoptive family competence, protection, understanding and practical advice. The presence of an understanding, caring and knowledgeable therapist makes it possible for individuals to accept feedback, develop insight and change behavior.

4. Valid Generalizations in Work With Adoptive Families

These conclusions are based on my years of experience with adoptive family therapy.

> • If the parents have a number of fine children and one child is causing problems in the family and at school, it is probably that child's problem, rather than a family scapegoating issue.

> • If a family has a number of children who are having problems in one way or another, the problem is probably parenting techniques.

> • The less strict parent needs to back the stricter — unless the stricter parent is verbally or physically abusive.

- The parent who had the happiest childhood is likely to have the most reliable "gut reaction" when handling children's problems.

- Parents set the upper limits for joy and self-image in their children.

- Therapy should not be done with a family when education will suffice. But time should not be wasted trying to educate the uneducable. Therapy should come first in these cases.

- No therapeutic intervention will help a family become healthier than the therapist.

- No adoption should be finalized unless both parents strongly favor finalization.

- It is vital to look at the total person. Physical illnesses affect mood and change personality traits. Therapists should look for physical illnesses first.

- Conservative methods of treatment should always be tried first.

- Genetics have greater influence on behavior than most therapists are willing to admit.

- If all helping professionals involved in a particular case are in radical disagreement, the child is likely a psychopath.

- The differences between neurotic, psychopathic and schizophrenic children are qualitative, not quantitative. A psychopath is *not* a very bad neurotic!

- Children with bonding and attachment problems generally show it most toward females.

- If things are going smoothly with an adolescent in treatment, it is likely that either the adolescent doesn't need the treatment or the therapist is being conned.

- If a child gets along well with parents through age 11 or sixth grade, it does not matter how badly adolescence proceeds, the child will probably grow up to be an adult, loving the parents and modeling them.

- Most parents and children can be treated effectively and economically in group.

5. *Overview of Therapeutic Intervention*

There are many effective methods of therapeutic intervention. However, increasing emphasis is being placed on cost effectiveness. Open-ended, week after week, ongoing and endless psychotherapy is definitely a thing of the past. Short-term therapy is the order of the day. In reaction to endless psychotherapy, the pendulum is probably swinging too far and many families who need more than short-term intervention are finding it difficult to receive third-party payments for more than six or eight visits. Moreover, most employee assistance programs or HMO groups now encourage therapists to see patients less, not more, and give the group monetary incentives for seeing the clients less frequently.

The teaching of practical parenting techniques has done more to help more families than any other single therapeutic intervention. Masses of individuals can be helped in a practical way and be provided support materials to reinforce basic concepts. Support materials may be either pamphlets, books or audio/video cassettes. Adoptive families may find support in a large number of cassettes that offer solutions for specific problems. Audio tapes that are available through the Cline/Fay Institute (P.O. Box 2362, Evergreen, CO, 80439) include:

- "Talking to Children about Child Abuse"
- "Talking to Children about Sex Abuse"
- "Talking to Children about Sex Play"
- "Trouble-free Teenagers"
- "Step-parenting Issues"
- "School Problems and Learning Disorders"
- "Talking to Children about Child Custody Issues"
- "Motivating Children for High Achievement"
- "My Best Friend Killed Himself—Talking to an Adolescent about Suicide of a Friend"

These high quality audio tapes were specifically designed to help adoptive and foster parents. Our Step Program likewise has provided parenting techniques to large numbers of people. Families can be helped effectively and economically in multimodal family groups. Parents learn from other parents under the guidance of an effective family therapist who is well versed in child development. Generally speaking, most children, most of the time, can be reached most effectively through their parents, who are with the child every day.

When education and multimodal family groups appear ineffective, individual psychotherapy with a child or parents is definitely indicated. Many adherents of individual child therapy believe that the impact made by the therapist in once-weekly or twice-weekly therapy sessions is more potent than impacting the children through the parents. A famous child therapist once said, in effect, "I can do more with children in one hour than the parents living with them do all week!" In general, the more disturbed the child, the more individual child therapy is both indicated and effective.

6. Examples of the Use of Varied Therapeutic Techniques

The Case for Parent Education—Wayne, the Child Afraid of Everything
Wayne, adopted at five, developed an allergic reaction to medication which at first was diagnosed as a neurologic problem, perhaps a brain tumor. Wayne was told that he had a brain tumor and went through a number of tests at a large children's hospital. Once the correct diagnosis was made and Wayne was taken off of the medication, his neurologic symptoms disappeared. However, Wayne began to develop fears of nearly everything. He was afraid he had AIDS. He was afraid of radioactive clouds drifting over the city. He was afraid to go to school. He was afraid to leave the house. These fears had gradually increased over the period of a year until Wayne, at age 11, was becoming a dysfunctional child. One session of parent education and a brief session with Wayne at the same time completely cleared up the problem.

The parents' reactions to Wayne's fears could be diagrammed as:

Mother:	Father:
Overprotective	Angry
Understanding	Consequential
Loving	Loving

The parents were told to take their individual strengths and combine them, and both to come through as consequential, loving and understanding. This may be diagrammed:

Mother:
    Consequential
    Understanding
    Loving

Father:
    Understanding
    Consequential
    Loving

Wayne's parents were also told that parents can never control a child's feelings. However, they can control the expression of the feelings toward the parents themselves. When Wayne had one of his "worry fits," the parents had said, "I'm sorry you feel that way, Wayne; we don't. Why don't you think about it in your room and when you're ready to come out and not hassle our heads with your fears, please do so." The parents were told that Wayne would resent that they did not commiserate with him more.

After only one session, an eighth-week follow-up showed that all of Wayne's fears had completely disappeared. His mother laughingly noted, "When Wayne said he was afraid the radioactive clouds would catch on fire and burn up the earth, I immediately got into my new gear and said, 'Well, Wayne, the good thing about that would be our all burning up together. No one would miss anyone else! However, if you still want to worry about that and talk about it, whip up to your room and when you're ready to think about something else, please do come out and join us for dinner.'"

The Case for Play Therapy — Ron's Fear of Surgery

Ron, a seven-year-old adopted at birth, was facing cardiac surgery for the second time. He was terrified. Directive play therapy about surgical techniques, with operation on a clay doll, completely relieved Ron's worries. He helped give the clay doll shots, connected him to IV's, and, with his therapist, wore a mask during the four play therapy sessions. Although previously terrorized by the surgical procedures, play therapy of this nature calmed his fears through familiarity and understanding.

The Case for Family Therapy — Gale Touched by her Father

Gale, the natural child of her mother, was adopted by her stepfather at age seven. At age 12, Gale reported that her father had fondled her sexually. The father admitted to this incident. In family therapy it was revealed that Gale's relationship to her mother was very distant. The only parent from whom Gale received any touch at all was her father. Gale tended to have a sibling/play-around relationship with her father, and the father's relationship with his wife was mother/child. These issues were easily seen in family therapy, and in a touching, confrontational and loving session Gale and her mother hugged each other, sobbing, telling each other of their wish for closeness and the difficulty they always had in finding it from each other. The mother told Gale about her poor relationship with her own mother and how she wanted this type of female generational conflict to disappear. The parents, seen in couple therapy, explored the reasons for their parent/child relationship and the poor sexual adjustment between them. Appropriate action was taken and the father was helped to become appropriately assertive and take on a parenting role with the children and a partner role with his wife. As the couple communicated around these issues, their sexual difficulties disappeared.

Family therapy was carried out in six sessions. Five years after the completion of family therapy, Gale wrote her therapist, "As nearly as I can tell now (Gale was leaving for college) my mother and father have a very loving and close relationship. Mom and I still get along very well and father and I have a loving but non-sexual!! relationship. Thank you again for helping our family talk to each other!"

The Case for Holding Therapy — Unbonded and Unattached Children

Recommending use of this therapy is drawn from several examples. Children who benefit from holding therapy might be four to twelve years old and might also be either hyperactive or controllingly passive. Such children generally show minimal eye contact. Parents, often adoptive or foster parents, describe the child's ability to relate through such statements as: "It's like living with the enemy," "It's like our love never mattered," or "When he was an infant, he never let me hold him — he always became stiff as a board." Children who have bonding and attachment problems almost always show excessive stealing, lying and cruelty to themselves or animals. One parent noted, "She takes joy in hurting little animals." Sometimes parents complain, "She acts loving on purpose. Her love isn't for us, it's a big act for others. When we are alone with her, there is no love at all, but when she is around other people, she's the most charming, loving child you can imagine!"

Children who have bonding and attachment problems almost always have a typical aberrant history during the first two years of life. Sometimes the children have been moved from home to home. Sometimes they have suffered pain the parents could not relieve. Sometimes there have been developmental difficulties requiring painful surgery. Sometimes the children have suffered abuse and neglect. As the children grow older, they manifest severe control problems, usually at home and at school.

Holding therapy is carried out on these touch-defensive children when other methods of treatment have not been effective and when the child has a typical history and typical symptoms. [Refer to Foster Cline's chapter in this book on intrusive therapies for a more complete description of holding.]

The TEAM Approach
Joan McNamara

Agencies and mental health practitioners have become aware of the unique issues involved in special-needs adoption and the need for specialized post-placement services. There is a growing awareness that these dynamics require resources with specific information and skills beyond traditional methods. The TEAM approach to adoption, as established by Tressler-Lutheran in Pennsylvania and the North American Council on Adoptable Children (NACAC), has outlined some of the critical support services needed, particularly in the framework of this difficult work with children. In addition, a number of programs around the United States have begun to address specifically the challenge of developing appropriate therapeutic resources.

While establishing its innovative special-needs adoption program in 1978, Family Resources found that families had significant difficulties in locating and utilizing community mental health services responsive to special-needs adoption. Family Resources, therefore, developed its own therapeutic component, integrated into the actual adoption process. Therapeutic services start right at recruitment, by providing information to adoptive families about the availability and necesssity of family supports in adoption and the understanding that all children and families at Family Resources participate in some form of therapeutic supports. The core of the post-placement program is a support network within which the therapy program works as part of a continuum of services.

Families making the commitment to adopting children with special needs at Family Resources contract at the beginning of the program for the eight-week adoptive parenting preparation course, Buddy Family visits and contacts, and both family and group therapy. The extensive parenting preparation for adoption involves prospective parents and experienced adoptive families with hands-on training in groups. The group is coordinated by a Family Resources staff member and an experienced adoptive parent. Part of the agenda is a discussion of the needs of children and parents in relation to the goals and process of therapy.

In addition to a panel of experienced parents sharing their

expertise during the training, an adoptive parent and child, usually a pre-teen or teen, may also join the group in a later session to talk about the actual experience of therapy. Therapists who will be working with the new families and their children also take part in this training, providing concrete information and insights, answering questions and establishing contacts for the future. Prospective parents become aware that painful issues for the children can stir up past issues for the adults, particularly concerning family relationships and sexuality. The need for parents to provide positive models for their children in facing difficult issues is explored, with both discussion and individual assessments by the prospective parents of how feelings such as sadness and anger are expressed and dealt with, personally and as a family.

As part of the preparation process, each new family is personally linked with its own Buddy Family, who has adopted a child or children similar to the children the new family hopes to adopt. In a home-visit to the Buddy Family, both concrete information and the intangible insights that come from experiential learning are gained. The Buddy Family contacts are continued through placement and beyond, providing informal peer counseling and social connections. One of the insights that may develop is the understanding that a child's negative behavior is not necessarily an indicator of bad parenting; parents can be doing a good job and providing excellent resources, yet a child may be unable to utilize them to change behavior patterns. For the experienced Buddy Family, sharing with new families reinforces that they have an expertise worth sharing, and reaffirms their skills and commitment.

With the help of these various supports, prospective families begin in the preparation group to develop more realistic expectations about children with special needs. Building on some basic understandings of child behavior as influenced by past traumas, families are more capable of anticipating reactions. They can then prepare to make appropriate responses and adaptations, slowly modifying their initial expectations and patterns. The advance contract made with families during the preparation process for adoption commits them to an informed and personal involvement with the multi-faceted support system at Family Resources. Emphasis is put on empowering the family, rather than reinforcing professional expertise. Parents and professionals are viewed as team members, and families are encouraged to make their own choices.

After the preparation process, families are urged to attend meetings to look at children in the adoption exchange books. Not only do these "book looks" provide opportunities to make choices and decisions about a wide range of specific children with special needs, but they also provide a more relaxed social setting and an opportunity to renew contacts with other waiting parents and staff. When a child is identified for a family, both adoption worker and therapist meet with the family. The team discusses the child's identified needs and behavior, the impact upon the family system and life style and what child issues are likely to collide with parental issues. They plan strategies for coping within the family and for therapy. Again, emphasis is on empowering the family and validating parental roles and the family/adoption choices. Parents are encouraged to use their Buddy Family.

Therapy is scheduled to begin immediately upon placement, usually within 48 hours. Therapy may start even before placement during a visit with the family, and includes the child's placement worker. With an older child, contracting is often done during the first therapy session. Initially, all family members participate in therapy. This varies later as different dynamics emerge. Since both children and parents have experienced loss and some loss of control in dealing with larger systems, opportunities for choices are made available.

Although the therapists working with Family Resources may vary in their therapeutic styles or philosophies, in general they share the same basic understandings of the dynamics of special-needs adoption and some of the more effective methods for dealing with these. The team concept, supportive of all team members, is one effective method. Therapy style tends to be direct, assertive, and at times confrontational. But it is also supportive, encouraging family strengths and relationships. It goes beyond dealing with problem behaviors to addressing the complex issues of separation and loss as they impact on all family members. Therapy is seen as a tool for bonding rather than a way to "fix things." Just as the family provides the child with a safe place to heal and bond, therapy provides opportunities to work through loss within a stable, secure, accepting environment.

Adoption is a precipitated crisis. Since crisis is time-limited, reaching a resolution or balance within a short period, Family

Resources tries to use this critical time to establish a new balance with an improved potential for growth of constructive family relationships. The initial resolution builds a base by opening up communications. Feelings about hurt need to be shared, accepted, acted upon in positive ways. The goal of therapy is to continue this constructive pattern of dealing with feelings, behaviors, and relationships in positive ways.

School-aged children participate in a bi-weekly teen or pre-teen therapy group. The group for younger children, meeting less often and using planned activities, focuses more on socialization and encouraging appropriate expression of feelings. For all of the children, group sessions provide another "safe place" to work, where they can connect with peers who share their traumas; they are no longer alone. There is group pressure to support one another, to belong. Parents are actively involved in these groups: before and after each group session, parents meet with the group therapists to discuss their feelings about the children's behaviors and needs, and the issues brought forth by the group. While the children are meeting, parents share in an informal support session.

In addition to post-placement family therapy and groups, the training sessions begun in preparation for adoption are continued after placement. The topics for "post-graduate" training are largely suggested or initiated by the needs of the families; such topics include sexual abuse, alcoholism, stress, residential services, fun ways to reinforce socialization skills, or developmental stages for adopted children. Adding to supportive connections are a parent-group newsletter, Buddy Family networking, camping trips and social activities, and informal respite care exchange between families. Regularly scheduled respite care rather than respite in response to crisis can help temper or avert burnout, crisis, or disruption for families. Parent volunteers are the significant factors in the success of these multi-faceted supports.

Parents adopting children with special needs usually lack the external supports from community and extended family generally available to biological parents. Lack of information, appropriate skills, an understood "etiquette" and the difficult behaviors of children themselves distance these traditional supports from families much in need of them. These families' experiences of parenting are different because the life experiences of their children have been different in traumatic ways. A program like Family Resources provides a sense of community acceptance combined with concrete information and skills. Connections with supportive professionals and peers reinforce commitments in practical ways. Many families say that the support network provides them with a new "extended family" where they feel welcome and strong.

A consistently low adoption disruption rate, 5% or under, with very high-risk special-needs children is only one measurement of significant success for the cost-effective Family Resources program. Family Resources' goal is to build not just intact families but healthy ones. This is much more difficult to assess. Feedback from families indicates overwhelmingly that the Family Resources approach supports them and encourages them to learn to integrate past experiences with present realities and resolve conflicts in ways that promote healthy development. Families with children who have special needs are not merely "hanging in there" but moving forward with a sense of strength. In this respect, Family Resources feels it has helped make adoption work.

Lifelong Issues in Adoption

Deborah N. Silverstein
Sharon Kaplan

Adoption is a lifelong, intergenerational process which unites the triad of birth families, adoptees, and adoptive families forever. Adoption, especially of adolescents, can lead to both great joy and tremendous pain. Recognizing the core issues in adoption is one intervention that can assist triad members and professionals working in adoption better to understand each other and the residual effects of the adoption experience.

Adoption triggers seven lifelong or core issues for all triad members, regardless of the circumstances of the adoption or the characteristics of the participants:

- loss
- rejection
- guilt and shame
- grief
- identity
- intimacy
- mastery/control

(Silverstein and Kaplan 1982).

Clearly, the specific experiences of triad members vary, but there is a commonality of affective experiences which persists throughout the individual's or family's life cycle development. The recognition of these similarities permits dialogue among triad members and allows those professionals with whom they interface to intervene in proactive as well as curative ways.

The presence of these issues does not indicate, however, that either the individual or the institution of adoption is pathological or pseudopathological. Rather, these are expected issues that evolve logically out of the nature of adoption. Before the recent advent of open and cooperative practices, adoption had been practiced as a win/lose or adversarial process. In such an approach, birth families lose their child in order for the adoptive family to gain a child. The adoptee was transposed from one family to another with time-limited and, at times, short-sighted consideration of the child's long-term needs. Indeed, the emphasis has been on the needs of the adults — on the needs of the birth family not to parent and on the needs of the adoptive family to parent. The ramifications of this attitude can be seen in the number of difficulties experienced by adoptees and their families over their lifetimes.

Many of the issues inherent in the adoption experience converge when the adoptee reaches adolescence. At this time three factors intersect: an acute awareness of the significance of being adopted; a drive toward emancipation; and a biopsychosocial striving toward the development of an integrated identity.

It is not our intent here to question adoption, but rather to challenge some adoption assumptions, specifically, the peristent notion that adoption is not different from other forms of parenting and the accompanying disregard for the pain and struggles inherent in adoption.

However, identifying and integrating these core issues into pre-adoption education, post-placement supervision, and all post-legalized services, including treatment, universalizes and validates triad members' experiences, decreasing their isolation and feelings of helplessness.

Loss

Adoption is created through loss; without loss there would be no adoption. Loss, then, is at the hub of the wheel. All birthparents, adoptive parents, and adoptees share in having expereinced at least one major, life-altering loss *before* becoming involved in adoption. In adoption, in order to gain anything, one must first lose — a family, a child, a dream. It is these losses and the way they are accepted and, hopefully, resolved which set the tone for the lifelong process of adoption.

Adoption is a fundamental, life-altering event. It transposes people from one location in the human mosaic into totally new configuration. Adoptive parents, whether through infertility, failed pregnancy, stillbirth, or the death of a child have suffered one of life's greatest blows prior to adopting. They have lost their dream child. No matter how well resolved the loss of bearing a child appears to be, it continues to affect the adoptive family at a variety of points throughout the family's love cycle (Berman and Bufferd 1986). This fact is particularly evident during the adoptee's adolescence when the issues of burgeoning sexuality and impending emancipation may rekindle the loss issue.

Birthparents lose, perhaps forever, the child to whom they are genetically connected. Subsequently, they undergo multiple losses associated with the loss of role, the loss of contact, and perhaps the loss of the other birthparent, which reshape the entire course of their lives.

Adoptees suffer their first loss at the initial separation from the birth family. Awareness of their adopted status is inevitable. Even if the loss is beyond conscious awareness, recognition, or vocabulary, it affects the adoptee on a very profound level. Any subsequent loss, or the perceived threat of separation, becomes more formidable for adoptees than their non-adopted peers.

The losses in adoption and the role they play in all triad members lives have largely been ignored. The grief process in adoption, so necessary for healthy functioning, is further complicated by the fact that there is no end to the losses, no closure to the loss experience. Loss in adoption is not a single occurrence. There is the initial, identifiable loss and innumerable secondary sub-losses. Loss becomes an evolving process, creating a theme of loss in both the individual's and family's development. Those losses affect all subsequent development.

Loss is always a part of triad members' lives. A loss in adoption is never totally forgotten. It remains either in conscious awareness or is pushed into the unconscious, only to be reawakened by later loss. It is crucial for triad members, their significant others, and the professional with whom they interface, to recognize these losses and the effect loss has on their lives.

Rejection

Feelings of loss are exacerbated by keen feelings of rejection. One way individuals seek to cope with a loss is to personalize it. Triad members attempt to decipher what they did or did not do that led to the loss. Triad members become sensitive to the slightest hint of rejection, causing them either to avoid situations where they might be rejected or to provoke rejection in order to validate their earlier negative self-perceptions.

Adoptees seldom are able to view their placement into adoption by the birthparents as anything other than total rejection. Adoptees even at young ages grasp the concept that to be "chosen" means first that one was "un-chosen," reinforcing adoptees' lowered self-concept. Society promulgates the idea that the "good" adoptee is the one who is not curious and accepts adoption without question. At the other extreme of the continuum is the "bad" adoptee who is constantly questioning, thereby creating feelings of rejection in the adoptive parents.

Birthparents frequently condemn themselves for being irresponsible, as does society. Adoptive parents may inadvertently create fantasies for the adoptee about the birth family which reinforce these feelings of rejection. For example, adoptive parents may block an adolescent adoptee's interest in searching for birthparents by stating that the birthparents may have married and had other children. The implication is clear that the birthparents would consider contact with the adoptee an unwelcome intrusion.

Adoptive parents may sense that their bodies have rejected them if they are infertile. This impression may lead the infertile couple, for example, to feel betrayed or rejected by God. When they come to adoption, the adoptors, possibly unconsciously, anticipate the birthparents' rejection and criticism of their parenting. Adoptive parents struggle with issues of entitlement, wondering if perhaps they were never meant to be parents, especially to this child. The adopting family, then, may watch for the adoptee to reject them, interpreting many benign, childish actions as rejection. To avoid that ultimate rejection, some adoptive parents expel or bind adolescent adoptees prior to the accomplishment of appropriate emancipation tasks.

Guilt/Shame

The sense of deserving such rejection leads triad members to experience tremendous guilt and shame. They commonly believe that there is something intrinsically wrong with them or their deeds that caused the losses to occur. Most triad members have internalized, romantic images of the American family which remain unfulfilled because there is no positive, realistic view of the adoptive family in our society.

For many triad members, the shame of being involved in adoption per se exists passively, often without recognition. The shame of an unplanned pregnancy, or the crisis of infertility, or the shame of having been given up remains unspoken, often as an unconscious motivator.

Adoptees suggest that something about their very being caused the adoption. The self-accusation is intensified by the secrecy often present in past and present adoption practices. These factors combine to lead the adoptee to conclude that the feelings of guilt and shame are indeed valid.

Adoptive parents, when they are diagnosed as infertile, frequently believe that they must have committed a grave sin to have received such a harsh sentence. They are ashamed of themselves, of their defective bodies, of their inability to bear children.

Birthparents feel tremendous guilt and shame for having been intimate and sexual; for the very act of conception, they find themselves guilty.

Grief

Every loss in adoption must be grieved. The losses in adoption, however, are difficult to mourn in a society where adoption is seen as a problem-solving event filled with joy. There are no rituals to bury the unborn children; no rites to mark off the loss of role of caretaking parents; no ceremonies for lost dreams or unknown families. Grief washes over triad members' lives, particularly at times of subsequent loss or developmental transitions.

Triad members can be assisted at any point in the adoption experience by learning about and discussing the five stages of grief: denial, anger, bargaining, depression, and acceptance (Kubler-Ross 1969).

Adoptees in their youth find it difficult to grieve their losses, although they are in many instances aware of them, even as young children. Youngsters removed from abusive homes are expected to feel only relief and gratitude, not loss and grief. Adults block children's expressions of pain or attempt to divert them. In addition, due to developmental unfolding of cognitive processes, adoptees do not fully appreciate the total impact of their losses into their adolescence or, for many, into adulthood. This delayed grief may lead to depression or acting out through substance abuse or aggressive behaviors.

Birthparents may undergo an initial, brief, intense period of grief at the time of the loss of the child, but are encouraged by well-meaning friends and family to move on in their lives and to believe that their child is better off. The grief, however, does not vanish, and, in fact, it has been reported that birth mothers may deny the experience for up to ten years (Campbell 1979).

Adoptive parents' grief over the inability to bear children is also blocked by family and friends who encourage the couple to adopt, as if children are interchangeable. The grief of the adoptive parents continues as the child grows up since the adoptee can never fully meet the fantasies and expectations of the adoptive parents.

Identity

Adoption may also threaten triad members' sense of identity. Triad members often express feelings related to confused identity and identity crises, particularly at times of unrelated loss.

Identity is defined both by what one is and what one is not. In adoption, birthparents are parents and are not. Adoptive parents who were not parents suddenly become parents. Adoptees born into one family, a family probably nameless to them now, lose an identity and then borrow one from the adopting family.

Adoption, for some, precludes a complete or integrated sense of self. Triad members may experience themselves as incomplete, deficient, or unfinished. They state that they lack feelings of well-being, integration, or solidity associated with a fully developed identity.

Adoptees lacking medical, genetic, religious, and historical information are plagued by questions such as: Who are they? Why were they born? Were they in fact merely a mistake, not meant to have been born, an accident? This lack of identity may lead adoptees, particularly in adolescent years, to seek out ways to belong in more extreme fashion than many of their non-adopted peers. Adolescent adoptees are overrepresented among those who join sub-cultures, run away, become pregnant, or totally reject their families.

For many couples in our society a sense of identity is tied to procreation. Adoptive parents may lose that sense of generativity, of being tied to the past and future, often created through procreation.

Adoptive parents and birthparents share a common experience of role confusion. They are handicapped by the lack of positive identity associated with being either a birthparent or adoptive parent (Kirk 1964). Neither set of parents can lay full claim to the adoptee and neither can gain distance from any problems that may arise.

Intimacy

The multiple, ongoing losses in adoption, coupled with feelings of rejection, shame, and grief as well as an incomplete sense of self, may impede the development of intimacy for triad members. One maladaptive way to avoid possible reenactment of previous losses is to avoid closeness and commitment.

Adoptive parents report that their adopted children seem to hold back a part of themselves in the relationship. Adoptive mothers indicate, for example, that even as an infant, the adoptee was "not cuddly." Many adoptees as teens state that they truly have never felt close to anyone. Some youngsters declare a lifetime emptiness related to a longing for the birthmother they may have never seen.

Due to these multiple losses for both adoptees and adoptive parents, there may also have been difficulties in early bonding and attachment. For children adopted at older ages, multiple disruptions in attachment and/or abuse may interfere with relationships in the new family (Fahlberg 1979 a,b).

The adoptee's intimacy issues are particularly evident in relationships with members of the opposite sex and revolve around questions about the adoptee's conception, biological and genetic concerns, and sexuality.

The adoptive parents' couple relationship may have been irreparably harmed by the intrusive nature of medical procedures and the scapegoating and blame that may have been part of the diagnosis of infertility. These residual effects may become the hallmark of the later relationship.

Birthparents may come to equate sex, intimacy, and pregnancy with pain leading them to avoid additional loss by shunning intimate relationships. Further, birthparents may question their ability to parent a child successfully. In many instances, the birthparents fear intimacy in relationships with opposite sex partners, family or subsequent children.

Mastery/Control

Adoption alters the course of one's life. This shift presents triad members with additional hurdles in their development, and may hinder growth, self-actualization, and the evolution of self-control.

Birthparents, adoptive parents, and adoptees are all forced to give up control. Adoption, for most, is a second choice. Birthparents did not grow up with romantic images of becoming accidentally pregnant or abusing their children and surrendering them for adoption. In contrast, the pregnancy or abuse is a crisis situation whose resolution becomes adoption. In order to solve the predicament, birthparents must surrender not only the child but also their volition, leading to feelings of victimization and powerlessness which may become themes in birthparents' lives.

Adoptees are keenly aware that they were not party to the decision which led to their adoption. They had no control over the loss of the birth family or the choice of the adoptive family. The adoption proceeded with adults making life-altering choices for them. This unnatural change of course impinges on growth toward self-actualization and self-control. Adolescent adoptees, attempting to master the loss of control they have experienced in adoption, frequently engage in power struggles with adoptive parents and other authority figures. They may lack internalized self-control, leading to a lowered sense of self-responsibility. These patterns, frequently passive/aggressive in nature, may continue into adulthood.

For adoptive parents, the intricacies of the adoption process lead to feelings of helplessness. These feelings sometimes cause adoptive parents to view themselves as powerless, and perhaps entitled to be parents, leading to laxity in parenting. As an alternative response, some adoptive parents may seek to regain the lost control by becoming overprotective and controlling, leading to rigidity in the parent/adoptee relationship.

Summary

The experience of adoption, then can be one of loss, rejection, guilt/shame, grief, diminished identity, thwarted intimacy, and threats to self-control and to the accomplishment of mastery. These seven core or lifelong issues permeate the lives of triad members regardless of the circumstances of the adoption. Identifying these core issues can assist triad members and professionals in establishing an open dialogue and alleviating some of the pain and isolation which so often characterize adoption. Triad members may need professional assistance in recognizing that they may have become trapped in the negative feelings generated by the adoption experience. Armed with this new awareness, they can choose to catapult themselves into growth and strength.

Triad members may repeatedly do and undo their adoption experiences in their minds and in their vacillating behaviors while striving toward mastery. They will benefit from identifying, exploring and ultimately accepting the role of the seven core issues in their lives.

The following tasks and questions will help triad members and professionals explore the seven core issues in adoption:

> • List the losses, large and small, that you have experienced in adoption.
>
> • Identify the feelings associated with these losses.
>
> • What experiences in adoption have led to feelings of rejection?
>
> • Do you ever see yourself rejecting others before they can reject you? When?
>
> • What guilt or shame do you feel about adoption? What feelings do you experience when you talk about adoption?
>
> • Identify your behaviors at each of the five stages of the grief process. Have you accepted your losses?
>
> • How has adoption impacted your sense of who you are?

Brief Solution-Focused Therapy with Adoptive Families

Judith Schaffer
Ron Kral

Adopted children and adolescents, though only an estimated two to four percent of the population, are thought to comprise a disproportionate number of referrals for mental health services. In a recent review of 5,135 patients registered for their first psychiatric services at a psychiatric facility in San Francisco, Brinich and Brinich (1984) found that representation of adoptees among Children's Service patients was somewhat higher than expected (5% against 2.2%), although representation of adoptees among adult patients (1.6%) was below the expected rate. Families who adopt infants are reported to be somewhat more likely than birthparents to seek professional help for parent/child difficulties. Nelson (1985) reported that 80 percent of her study families who had adopted special-needs children cited a need for mental health services that were timely, specialized, sensitive and competent as their greatest need. While it is apparent that adoptees and their families contend with a number of difficulties and added tasks associated with this status, it is not at all clear that these difficulties result in psychopathology (Tienari, et al. 1987; Brodzinsky, et al. 1985; Bohman 1982).

Kral, Schaffer and deShazer (1987) therefore recommend that clinicians treating adoptees and their families distinguish between adoption-related difficulties, many of which need to be seen as normal and accepted as such; problems that in fact are adoption-related and require adoption-specific treatment; and usual parent/child problems which may not be related to adoption. They further caution the therapist against doing too much. They recommend that treatment progress in small steps with the open expectation that the solution may be reached at any point. Therefore, psychologists, psychiatrists, clinical social workers, mental health counselors, family therapists, nurses and school personnel will have to develop a greater understanding of the needs of adopted individuals and their families, along with an understanding of the normal difficulties associated with this status, in order to help them effectively.

Adoption is a family issue. It can affect both the way parents view their role (Feigelman and Silverman 1979; Kirk 1964) and how adoptees see themselves (Lifton 1979). It can color the ways in which family members interact with each other and with other systems such as schools, health care facilities, extended families and institutions. Treating the adoptive family requires sensitivity to more than the psychology of an individual adoptee. It requires educating parents about the normal course of child development along with the unique developmental tasks of the adopted child. It may also necessitate actively convincing adoptive parents that they possess the necessary skills, attitudes and abilities to raise adopted children successfully.

Since the early 1980's, the Center for Adoptive Families (CAF)[1] in New York City and the Brief Family Therapy Center (BFTC)[2] in Milwaukee have been investigating the elements of effective "solution-focused", brief therapy with adoptive families. The two mental health treatment facilities collected data on 180 adoptive families over the course of four years. Families either chose one of these agencies or were referred by an outside source for specialized treatment relating to adoption. This sample is not considered representative of adoptive families in general, since the vast majority of adoptees and their families do not seek mental health services (Schaffer and Kral 1988).

An adoptive family was defined as containing at least one parent and legally adopted child not related by blood or marriage. Families with children adopted as infants (30%) were combined with those where the child was placed at two years and above (70%). The mean age of adoptive placement for older child placements was eight years. In all of the cases the adopted child was presented as the identified patient (IP). The mean age of the IP was 11.6 years at the time of treatment. The most common (modal) ages of IP's were 13 and 14 years. No significant difference was noted in mean ages at time of treatment

---

[1] The treatment team at the Center for Adoptive Families in New York City has included, at various times, Judith Schaffer, Christina Lindstrom, Arnold Frucht, Mary Walker, Mary Talen, Anne Hoerning, Mary Ann Yanulis, Helen Hazan, Jeanne Warnock, Trish Welsh and Marie Ryan.

[2] The treatment team at the Brief Family Therapy Center in Milwaukee includes Ron Kral, Steve de Shazer, Insoo Kim Berg, Karen Berge and Kate Kawalski.

between the infant placements (treated at mean 11.8 years) and the older child placements (mean 11.5 years).

Sixty-nine percent of the IP's were either oldest or only children. The majority of the families and children seen in New York were either black or Hispanic. In Milwaukee, the majority were white families who had adopted either white or Asian youngsters.

The problems present in all but seven of the cases were related to conduct or externalized behaviors, such as school difficulties, lying, sexual acting-out, stealing, aggressive behavior, noncompliance, running away, drug abuse, and rude behavior. The remaining cases involved adoption-specific issues, such as a parent telling a three-year-old child that she was adopted or the development of the family relationship when an adolescent was adopted.

Sixty-three percent of the families included two parents. In New York, unmarried individuals accounted for 39 percent of the families who had adopted older children. Single-parent families accounted for only a small number of the families who had adopted infants, and were usually the result of death or divorce. Twenty percent of the single parents were men.

The average number of therapy sessions was 7. Single-parent families averaged 8 sessions. Infant placements averaged 5.7 sessions while the mean for older child placements was 7.5. Early information, based on follow-up of 20 percent of the families, as well as our own clinical impressions, suggest that nearly three-fourths of these clients report that they are doing better than they were before, their goals for therapy were met, and the presenting complaint has not reoccurred. A more intensive follow-up is currently underway.

Although nearly 30 percent of the parents who had adopted older children came in considering adoption dissolution as a solution to their difficulties, only a small percentage of these did so (3.8 percent). Three additional cases resulted in some kind of temporary out-of-home placement (residential treatment, psychiatric hospitalization or boarding school) without termination of parental rights and with continued parental involvement.

Brief Therapy
    The adoptive family cases were all treated using the Brief, Solution-Focused Model described by deShazer (1985) and deShazer, et al. (1986). This model has been influenced by the

work of Milton Erickson and assumes that people have within them the natural abilities to overcome difficulties. The work of therapy is therefore to elicit rather than teach new abilities. O'Hanlon (1986:7-20) has summarized the following basic assumptions of Erickson and therapists influenced by him:

1. It is not necessary to know the cause of symptoms or problems, since one can never know with any certainty, the cause of any human situation.

2. Insight and awareness are not necessary for change. The unconscious is the essential part of all psychological functioning.

3. Preconceptions about patients hamper therapists.

4. People can change behavior (the visible expression of personality).

5. Symptoms are not necessarily expressions of underlying problems or past traumas. They may once have had a function but now may just be a habit pattern.

Principles of Brief Solution-Focused Therapy.
   The overriding principle in Brief Therapy is its adherence to a nonpathological view of families and individuals. Problems are seen as a result of ineffective patterns of interactions between members/elements of a system, and these patterns are seen as the result of "bad luck." That is, due to some chance occurrence, a pattern of behavior or perception develops and is maintained by habit instead of by deeper, psychological reasons. Therefore, the "task of Brief Therapy is to help clients do something different, by changing their interactive behavior and/or their interpretation of behavior and situations so that a solution (the resolution of their complaint) can be achieved," (deShazer 1985:208). This change process is aided by the apparent fact that clients bring into therapy personal resources that can be utilized. More importantly, however, clients are seen as continually learning and changing, usually in ways of which they are unaware. Therefore, the therapist need not initiate change, only discover and accentuate positive changes that are already in process.

   Example: The M family came into treatment because their only child, a 15-year-old adopted daughter, who had previously been "perfect," refused to go to school, was failing all of her courses, and had become rude and often violent with her parents. When asked to do something she would refuse and scream, "You can't make me do it! You are not my real mother!" The parents took this to heart, felt that they had failed to make their daughter secure and responded by being more solicitous of her feelings, continually assuring her of their love. They also decreased the numbers of demands they made of her. The increased expressions of love and the decrease in limits only made the problem worse, and so the M's next began to worry about the possibility of certain genetic vulnerabilities, since their daughter's mother had given birth to her when she was 15. These parents, who had formerly been successful, came to believe that they were incompetent to raise an adopted adolescent.

The M's met with a pscyhoanalyst and were told that virtually all adoptees suffer from low self-esteem because of rejection by their birthmothers. The task of therapy in this case was to interrupt a problematic pattern of interaction. The parents had set effective limits for their daughter when she was younger and probably needed to do so again, taking into account the fact that she was an adolescent. The M's further benefited from adoption-specific treatment that assumed that they were competent parents who had raised, if anything, an overconfident daughter. The daughter's angry references to "real" parents, while having some obvious merit, were assumed to be a bad habit that she had developed, and had been sustained by interaction with parents who felt insecure about raising an adolescent, especially an adopted one. The M's were assured that there was no research-based information that would link their daughter's behavior with her genetic background and a great deal that would link it with family interaction. The problem was resolved in three sessions. It was not necessary to address any further adoption-related issues at that time, since neither the M's nor their daughter wished to do so. Three years following treatment, the parents report that their daughter attends a college away from home, and that the family "survived" their daughter's adolescence as well as most of their friends survived with their children who were not adopted.

Concrete evidence of a viable solution are elicited in therapy as "exceptions." An exception is a point in time or situation when the problem behavior could have occurred, but did not. Therapy focusses on what the client did and/or thought at those times and how that exception can be elicited. In cases where the clients are unable to describe exceptions, tasks are assigned which assist the client in discovering them (for example see deShazer and Molnar 1984).

> *Example:* Mrs. L brought her 15-year-old daughter in for treatment for a continuing problem of bedwetting. Ever since her adoptive placement at the age of five, Becky had wet her bed, every single night without exception. Most kinds of medical treatment and several kinds of psychotherapy had been tried over the years and nothing had worked. Mrs. L was concerned that this was a sign of Becky's history of cruel sexual abuse by her birthfather, which had culminated in her removal from her birth family by the police when she was four years old. If this was the case, as some professionals she had seen had suggested, then how would it be possible to resolve this difficulty, since Becky's past would always be a part of her life? Mrs. L was becoming hopeless, and so was Becky.
>
> The therapist sought exceptions to this pattern of bedwetting from Becky. There were no exceptions. Feeling stuck, the therapist went behind the one-way mirror to consult with the team. The team suggested that the therapist no longer discuss the bedwetting, but instead focus on the times when Becky could control her bladder. The therapist began to question Becky about how she was able to control her bladder during the day. Becky was able to do so with ease and never had accidents. In fact, she disliked the girl's room so much in her school, that she usually controlled her bladder from 7:30 a.m. to 4:30 p.m. every day.
>
> The message from the team congratulated Becky for having such remarkable control of her bladder. Becky was asked to observe, so that she could describe to the team the next time, how she was able to control her bladder during the day. The new pattern of noting the "exceptions" was powerful enough to increase Becky's

control of her bladder during the night. During the week she was able to control her bladder for four nights. The following week she was able to control her bladder for five nights. Therapy was terminated in four sessions when Mrs. L and Becky stated that they no longer believed there was a problem in this area.

Clients are also viewed from a position of cooperation (deShazer, et al. 1986; deShazer 1985). This concept maintains that clients cooperate with therapy in a variety of ways. The therapist's job is to identify the client's unique style of cooperation and then to cooperate in a fashion which will support continued progress in therapy. In practice this requires that the family's view of the problem be understood and the goals they set accepted. Therapy focuses upon what the clients do or think that is useful for them, and merely ignores the failures. In this manner, clients are not expected to learn entirely new patterns of interacting, only to do more of what they are already doing or have been able to do in the past that includes a solution to the present complaint, or at least might prompt a solution.

Example: The W family came into treatment because of a serious difficulty with Missy, their adopted seven-year-old daughter, that was causing them to consider terminating the adoption. They had first consulted their pediatrician, who had referred them to a psychiatrist. Both physicians recommended that Missy be returned to her agency and the adoption dissolved because of deep psychopathology not amenable to treatment. Missy, who had spent the first five years of her life in foster care, had apparently been sexually abused regularly in her foster home. Although the agency was not aware of this and therefore did not inform the W's of this problem, as Missy began to feel comfortable with her new adoptive family she began to talk about her past experience. Yet the W's reported that Missy had done quite well at home, in the community and at school. Then, two years following her adoption, Missy and her brother were discovered having sexual intercourse. Following the advice of the physicians, who viewed Missy as the aggressor, the W's contacted their former agency and were referred for adoption-specific treatment.
The therapist decided to ignore the dire predictions

which the W's had been given and proceed as if there would be a solution to the problem of sexual activity between siblings. As the therapist questioned the parents about their activities since the incident, it soon became apparent to both the family and the team that no sexual behavior had occurred since the original incident and the parents had taken steps at home so that this could not happen again. No further change had to be elicited through therapy. Instead, Missy, her brother and their parents needed to become aware that the problem had already been resolved. Missy's former experience was a fact that could not be altered. Her interactional difficulties had already been resolved.

The W's were complimented on their activities since the incident and encouraged to continue this approach. The family was advised that the team considered the problem resolved and that Missy and her brother would need to be taught more appropriate ways of demonstrating their caring. In the two years following treatment, the W's report that there has been no recurrence of this behavior and that Missy continues to do well in all aspects of her life.

In the process of encouraging changes, several other basic principles are applied. Since the problematic pattern is held within the context of a system, only a small change in any part of the system can be sufficient to bring about a significant and lasting solution. This can mean that the "problem child" may never have to come for treatment if his or her parents do, since change in an aspect of the way the parents interact with him or her concerning the problem behavior can potentially result in a resolution of the problem. It further means that issues from a former foster child's abused and neglected past may not have to be discussed and/or resolved in treatment for his or her behavior to change and for family relationships to improve. This principle frees the therapist from doing too much. Rather, therapy progresses in small steps with an open expectation that the solution may be reached at any point—it only needs to be recognized and firmly established over time. Consequently, the therapy is brief in the sense of a limited number of sessions. The total time may be over several months, as the clients are given ample time to test and adapt to changes in the context of their situation.

Format of Brief Solution-Focused Therapy Sessions

A review of the format of brief solution-focused therapy is presented below. Readers are encouraged to refer to deShazer (1985), and deShazer et al. (1986) for a more complete description of the model.

Families and individuals are seen by a treatment team made up of several therapists, one in the room with the client and one or more behind a one-way mirror. Most therapy sessions are videotaped with the clients' consent, and these videotapes are used for treatment, research and training. In the first session the following format is used:

1. Introduction

2. Statement of the complaint

3. Exploration of exceptions to the complaint

4. Establishment of goals for therapy

5. Definition of potential solutions

6. Consultation break

7. Delivery of the message from the team

1. Introduction

In the first session, the client is introduced to the set-up. The therapist describes the one-way mirror, consulting team and videotaping equipment. A few minutes are spent getting to know one another—how old the children are, which ones are adopted, where they live, what schools they go to, and so forth.

2. Statement of the Complaint

The therapist then asks "What can I help you with?" or, "What brings you in?" The therapist extracts, step-by-step, facts of the problematic pattern or complaint sequence. The therapist asks questions to elicit who is most invested in resolving the difficulty. Often this person is a parent and therapy may be focused solely on getting this person to do something different. Here, the therapist has an opportunity to "normalize" certain behaviors the family may consider pathological. For example, most adopted children test what their parents will do with statements such as, "You're not my REAL mother!". The therapist will also "reframe" or alter the meaning the family applies to a set of observable events, giving a positive rather than negative flavor to them. Examples, such as referring to acting-out on the part of a recently placed child as "testing behavior because the child is beginning to feel secure," or "slow to warm up" or "withdrawn," can be used to alter slightly the client's perception and to help set the stage for other interventions.

3. Exceptions

The next phase of the interview is designed to find out what happens when the problem behavior could happen and does not. Both the therapist and clients need to know what the clients do that is effective.

4. Goals

Concrete goals are elicited from the client to provide a way to measure the usefulness of therapy. The goals help to build the expectation that change is going to happen. Concrete goals also are a necessary part of follow-up or outcome studies.

5. Solutions

Clients are asked, "How will you know when the problem is solved?" and "What will be different once the problem is a part of your past?" When alternate futures or alternate solutions are talked about, the clients' expectations of change become greater.

6. Consultation Break

During this ten-minute break, while the family waits in the treatment room, the team and therapist decide what to do and how to do it. Therapists working without teams also excuse themselves to review their notes and gather their thoughts.

A message is developed and has two parts: Compliments and Clues. Compliments are based on what the client is doing already that is useful or good or right in some way. They are designed to help the client develop a more flexible view of the situation, thereby enabling a solution to begin developing. The goal is to help clients see themselves as normal persons with normal difficulties. Clues are focused on therapeutic suggestions, tasks, or directives about other things the clients might do that will likely be good for them and lead toward a solution.

7. Message Delivery

After the intermission, the therapist returns and gives the formal intervention. This message is written down for the therapist to read. Perhaps because the clients have been kept waiting, their receptiveness seems increased. A formula task often used in the first session is, "Between now and the next time we meet, we would like you to observe, so that you can describe it to us next time, what happens in your life that you want to continue to have happen."

Second and Subsequent Sessions

In subsequent sessions the therapist focuses on those things that are happening that should continue. As each item or sequence is mentioned, the therapist wonders aloud if it is "new" or "different." The therapist then shifts from the notion that these things have just "happened" to "How did you get them to happen?"

If the client reports no improvement, the therapist will ask questions again about what it is that the client is doing that is working. This search for exceptions will continue by saying, "It is our experience that if people don't do something right, things will get worse over time rather than remain the same. What are you doing?"

If the situation is deteriorating, the therapist asks: "Have things hit bottom and you can reasonably expect them to get better soon? Or, have things yet to hit bottom and so they won't get better so quickly?" Homework tasks would be focused on signs of current improvement or continuing deterioration.

Provided things are reported as "better," the interval between sessions is lengthened from once a week to once every two or three weeks, and then to once every six weeks, giving the client(s) time to test and adapt to changes.

CASE EXAMPLE: "Three Coins"

The Whites came into therapy with their 12-year-old adopted son, Billy. He was one of four children living at home and one of 14 children in the White family. Ten children had been adopted by the Whites as older or special-needs placements. Mrs. White wanted therapy for Billy because he had recently stolen $65 from her purse. This was the fourth incident of stealing since he was adopted three years earlier. Each of the previous incidents involved large sums of money as well, including a portion of the rent money a year earlier. She told the therapist that Billy always denied that he stole the money, even when it was found on him or in his things. When he had money, he would buy things for other children, like candy or small toys. Mrs. White appeared to be very distraught, as "none of the other children had ever stolen anything." She said she had been warned by Billy's foster mother that he stole things and that his birthfather had been a thief. "People inherit things like that, you know!" she said. Here was an example of highly experienced and competent parents paralyzing themselves. The frame to which they attributed Billy's behavior was "bad blood." This meant that from their perspective there was nothing that they or Billy could do to stop the stealing; it was inevitable. Therapy therefore had to be concerned with altering this frame, "reframing" Billy's behavior in such a way that his parents and/or he could control it. The therapist's attempts both to elicit exceptions to the rule by discussing what occurred between the stealing incidents, and to reframe the behavior as "learned" and therefore amenable to being "unlearned," were met with the parents' references to Billy's past and his "inheritance." When Mr. White stated that they would know the problem was solved when money could be safely left out, his wife scolded him for saying this in front of the boy. Throughout the session, Billy sat rather passively and responded to his mother's direct question, "Why did you take the money?" with, "I don't know."

The team sent the following message to the family after the break: "We are impressed with how polite and attentive you were during this session. Most other teenagers would not have been able to do that. It seems to us that you do care about your parents.

"We need more information about this complex and serious problem so that we can be helpful to you. We will need some further information about the things that are going on in your family that you do not want to have us work on — the things that are going well, especially where Billy is concerned. Between now and the next time we meet, we would therefore like you to observe, so that you can describe it to us next time, what happens in your family that you want to continue to have happen."

Upon hearing this message, Mrs. White spontaneously described Billy as a kind, helpful boy who was good most of the time.

The second session began with a list of many positives about Billy and some perceived changes. Billy's sister said that he had helped with the dishes without being asked, something new for him. Mrs. White appeared more relaxed and less upset about the stealing incident. She again asked Billy why he stole. This time he stated that he had a "little voice" in his head that told him not to steal and he usually listened to it. The therapist observed that it probably was like a little transistor radio, that sometimes just needed to be turned up a little louder so Billy could hear it better. The remainder of this session revolved around the many good things which Billy and other family members were doing at home.

The Whites were told by the team: "We are impressed with the many good things going on in your family. That was useful for us to know. We are now convinced that Billy has a conscience, the little voice he hears. It seems to us that his conscience needs some adjustment, since he is not always able to hear it, even when he would like to. We need just a bit more information about his conscience before we can decide what needs to be done, so we would like you to get two jars. One should be empty and the other should be filled with 100 pennies. Every night, before he goes to bed, Billy should move one penny from the full jar to the other one for every time he was tempted to do something wrong and then listened to his conscience." Both Billy and his parents seemed pleased with this idea and left the session discussing where they could find the jars.

The next session was two weeks later. Billy came in carrying a jar with only a few pennies in it. The therapist asked Billy about the jar. He said that these were the times he listened to his conscience. Upon counting them, the therapist remarked that there were only three pennies in there. Mrs. White immediately responded, "He was only tempted three times." Billy agreed that he, indeed, was only tempted three times and that he had listened to his conscience each time. Mrs. White indicated that the positive behaviors she had noted in Billy last time had continued, and she was beginning to trust the boy more.

The team's message complimented the family on the continued positive changes and noted what a powerful conscience Billy has. The team supported Mrs. White's increasing trust, and cautioned that progress can slip sometimes, but that things certainly seemed to be going in the right direction, a statement she immediately agreed with. The Whites were told that there did not seem to be anything else the team could do for them at that time, but if further help was needed they should make another appointment. A follow-up call several months later indicated that Billy was still listening to his conscience and money was safe at the White's. Two years following treatment, Mr. and Mrs. White report that Billy's conscience continues to improve and that their usual methods of discipline work as effectively with Billy as with their other children.

The White case demonstrates a rather common problem with older adoptions, the possibility of inherited or background problems. Using the Brief Therapy model, the team avoided addressing this as the problem, while they listened to the family's concerns. Instead, therapy focused on a solution— Billy's conscience and how he used it. Even with "bad blood," Billy had a conscience that was working, for the most part. Therapy simply needed to increase its efficiency while pointing out the existence of the conscience to Mr. and Mrs. White. In this case, the simplicity of this approach resulted in positive results (Kral and Schaffer 1988).

Conclusion

Although adoptees and their families have been character-ized as suffering from inherent difficulties which put them "at risk" for psychopathology, our clinical experience and prelimi-nary investigations suggest that, as a group, those who enter treatment at CAF and BFTC are very responsive to brief solu-tion-focused therapy. The complicated nature of these families, especially those who have adopted older children, requires that the therapist make distinctions carefully about what to focus on during treatment, and what not to focus on (Kral, Schaffer and deShazer 1987). The therapist can be tempted to do "too much," more than the family is in fact requesting. As clinicians, the teams have been satisfied that the methods we have presented are useful in helping clients meet and/or exceed the goals set at the start of therapy. To meet the standards of scientific rigor further, more objective follow-up needs to be reported in the future.

We as therapists do not seek to deny the very real difficul-ties for adoptees that are a natural result of the secrecy that surrounds their birth backgrounds and that has been supported by law and public policy. Family therapists are uniquely aware of the negative effects of "secrets" on family interactions. Simi-larly, we are aware of the tragic life histories of many former foster children now being placed for adoption, and how these early experiences color their current family interactions. We have consciously worked to acknowledge the very real difficulties that may face adoptive families and adoptees, in the process of providing useful assistance for change. We have confined this report to a treatment approach that we have found useful in helping families with children resolve the problems that they brought into therapy, in a brief and respectful manner.

Treating Older Adoptees:
An Interview with Claudia Jewett

The following is excerpted from an interview conducted by University of Southern Maine research staff with author and therapist Claudia Jewett of Harvard, Massachusetts on May 29, 1987, and reflects her experiences treating troubled adoptees.

USM: What can you tell us about your method and philosophy for treating older adopted children and their families?

CJ: There are several things that I believe are important for people to know. Everything youngsters do or say, either behaviorally or in words signals to us *why* they're doing what they're doing: they do it because at some time it worked. When kids come into my office, if I make a space for them, they are going to show or tell me, given their level of conception, where they've learned the behavior that's no longer working. Then my job is to help the youngster understand that they do make perfect sense, that the behavior or thought pattern that they followed at one time was true and worked; but that things have changed around them, so it's giving them a hard time. We need to find out how they can have that need or feeling taken care of. We're not trying to change what they think or how they feel. We're not trying to tell them they shouldn't need what they need. All we're trying to do is tell them they deserve to not have a hard time getting their thoughts and needs and feelings addressed in an appropriate way.

That's the basic theory with which I'm working. I have not seen children for whom that was not true, and I've seen thousands of children. I absolutely believe that most of what we label pathology in kids has a beginning place. The kid, or his or her history, can tell you where the beginning place was. Then, given this child's outlook on life, what's happened and when, it becomes a question of how you can take his or her ability to cope and survive and turn it into something that works better.

That's what I do, and in a variety of ways. I don't waste any time. Any youngster under ten or eleven who comes into my office will be told that this is a place with very few rules. The rules are:

1. No one intentionally puts anybody down (including themselves) about what they think and feel.

2. Nobody speaks for anybody else. They speak only about their own thoughts and feelings and needs.

3. Nobody hits anyone.

4. Nobody intentionally breaks things in here. Now, sometimes things get broken because people are working on a feeling that's much more important than what gets broken. But if they were to decide, for example, to pick up a chair and throw it through my window, I would be very angry about that.

5. We take turns at being boss. They will have equal time: half the time they will be boss, and half the time I will. There is a timer in the closet, and if we need to use the timer at the beginning until they trust how we work, I'm happy to get it.

With my turn, I'm going to get right to the issues. I'm going to start out by doing projective testing, so that I can get some good suggestions from the kid. Before they come, I will usually have done my homework and taken history. If it's a kid who's not coming to me from an agency but from the family, I will see the parents first and take a history from the parents. What I want to know in the history is what they think is important, because what they include and what they leave out tells me an awful lot about what's happening in the family.

I want to spend that first session so that parents understand that, in addition to the children in their family, there is a child in each one of them. That child is in pain, and that's why they're here. I recognize that the pain and the children in them are as important to me as the child they're bringing to see me. They get equal time and have equal rights to having their own thoughts and needs taken care of, and I will make a contract with them that that will happen in this phase.

I do not keep secrets from parents, usually. My preference is to have parents in the session with kids, even with adolescents, because it doesn't waste time. When you say to a resistant adolescent, "So how are things going?", they can say, "Fine" for weeks. If their parents are here, they can't say, "Fine" for weeks because their parents are going to say, "Baloney."

In addition to that all the kids that I work with have had lots of losses. The kids I see connect to me very tightly. They trust me quickly because I do let them be boss. I really want to take the hassle out of their lives, and that comes across in my approach. So, they tell me what their hassles are, where the pain is. We try to piece together where that came from. But I don't intend to take any of the children home who come to my office. And I don't want to work hard with them to form a therapeutic alliance with me and do a lot of transference. I want them to do that with their parents, and that's why I want their parents here. When a child reveals something to me that makes sense, I want the parents to hear it. I also want them to know how we got to the point that the kid could tell us, because parents don't know how to do that; nobody's trained them. Parents say to kids, "Why did you do that?" Kids can't answer a question when it's asked that way; that's not how they think. But there are ways that you can ask them that they can tell you. They understand exactly what they were feeling and needing, and once the parents understand, they begin to change quickly, because they know that they don't have a crazy kid, they just have a kid who's trying to survive.

They also have a chance to draw some modeling from me, such as: "How do you confront a kid in a way that's loving? That says I really am on your team, and we need to talk about this? It's going to be really hard for you to talk about, and it may be embarrassing, and what's the best way to go about it? Shall we just jump in and get it over with? Do we need to ease into it?" What happens with the families I work with, by and large, is that we'll know we're through when the parents become better therapists to their child than I am, because they have the kid all week long. And I'm going to try very hard to stay out of the middle of that. Sometimes I work by getting both parents and the kid angry at me instead of at each other, so that they can align together, because I don't mind people being angry at me.

So I use my turn to get down to brass tacks. What I want to address is, "Where does it hurt and how can we fix it? Why do you keep giving yourself this hassle? Do you want to do something about it? If you don't, where and how did you learn that you're not worth taking care of? You are worth taking care of, and (usually) there are three people in this office who think so. I think you've got a wrong idea there, and one of my wishes is for you to change that wrong idea."

If I have a kid who can't take positive ideas, who puts himself down, I call him every single time he does it. I say, "You may not do that to yourself. One of the rules in this office is that people do not put people down, including themselves, for what they think and how they feel." We create a very safe haven.

I don't have anything in my closet that isn't going to be therapeutic. I don't play checkers with kids because I don't learn anything. I do learn from playing the *Ungame* game with kids and families, and they learn about each other: fun things, scary things, ways in which they're alike and different. With adolescents and with kids, sometimes when we're working on family history it's been a good-bye, how the good-bye was done or said, that has started the behavior that's giving the kids a hassle. So very often we're working on some historical things: "What do you think happened in your life? If you could do it differently, and have a different ending, how could it get that ending? Is that really realistic? If you got the different ending, how would it be good for you?" We're going to talk about the fantasies so that I can understand them. "How can you have this family and your other family and not lose anybody at all?" Sometimes we're going to do that for real, actually reconnect people so nobody loses anybody. But sometimes that's not appropriate.

When I'm working with history, I say to kids of all ages that much has been written down about their history, and yet they were not the person who wrote it down. I push that very hard with adolescents. I will say something like, "You know, I looked at your history. It's three inches thick. For X number of years of your life, people have been writing down things about you, and you never had a chance to have a say. This is your chance. I want to go through what do you believe happened in your life, and what the record says happened in your life. What needs to be corrected and what's been left out that's important? It's your turn now to be in charge." What I try to do is allot empowerment, and that attracts adolescents because they like being empowered. They like having a chance to have their say, and they deserve that chance.

I also do that with younger children. I'm working with a six-year-old and a nine-year-old, doing the same sort of thing. We're working on behavior and symbols so that they can tell me what they need to do about some very painful issues. Many of the children and adolescents I see are stuck in two big places. One is that they have been helpless. People have said, "This is where you're living, until we whip you away from there. This is who you can love. Now you can never see them again." They need to have a say about how they feel about what's happened, and they need to know that there are things they have the right to think about, to feel about, to make choices about.

There are other things that are not their choice; that's part of life. What can they do about that? They can take as much time as they need, because they are entitled to their feelings. But the truth remains that the feelings are not going to make a difference. There is no way I believe that they can have what they want, and sometimes I tell them I think that really rots, because what they want would be really good. But it's not something I can deliver or that I think they can get on their own. I think they're spending an awful lot of energy trying to get something they can't get, and it would make more sense for them to just say, "I have to make peace with the fact that's not going to happen." And I think that's something they can do. That involves some grieving, so a lot of the work I do is on grieving.

The other place that kids get stuck is what we now believe is a lifetime, developmental issue for everyone: the swing between merging and individuating. How much are you going to be your own person, and how lonely will you have to be to do that? How much will you compromise yourself in order to merge cooperatively with another person? Children are on that swing at a much faster tempo. In an adult lifespan, we're talking about seven years; but that doesn't begin until about 23. Kids are on much shorter cycles. Kids who have suffered losses have huge issues around closeness and distance. In adolescents, one of the biggest problems is the pattern of their loss. They have to individuate; that's one of their developmental tasks. They also have to merge with a peer group, and it's terrifying because they equate being close with being out of control, with being engulfed. They know they haven't completed their dependency issues, but they have to leave home. Maybe they're not ready to leave home in the same way at the same time as other people. They don't know what to do with that, so they get into big trouble, and they leave home very precipitously. They leave home too early, to get it over with, in the same way that they have sex too early to get it over with, because it's just so complicated they don't know what to do. Their ambivalence about merging and individuating is very high. Most of them have had a sudden, unexpected, ambivalent loss, which is the very worst kind. There was no dead body, because the person continued to live, so there was no actual grief. That really complicates grieving. So they've had very complicated grieving to do, when they didn't have a lot of developmental skills to do it.

Now they're getting ready for graduation, which is why people like me are so busy this time of year. It suddenly occurs to them that for twelve years they have been merging, making close friends with teachers, coaches, kids, the system, and the rules. They've subjugated their individuality, because it's not safe to be an individual in most high schools. And the payoff for that's graduation, and they've been gearing up for that all year long. They're seniors. They're going to have class day and skip day, they're going to have a yearbook with their individual picture, they're going to be heard at last on class day. And the next day they're going to graduate, and by the end of class day it will have dawned on them that the reward for what they've done for twelve years is to lose everything at once. For most of the kids I see, that's how all of their losses have been. So adolescence becomes a very volatile time, because to do what they need to do they have to give up some dependency they're not ready to give up. They expect, since it's the pattern, that they can't leave home without losing everything; and they get really scared. So, most of the kids I see come across very bravado and contrived, very, "I don't need nothing from no grown-ups." They're terrified of the total dependency and they're terrified of the loss. They don't want to get close to anyone else because they know what the payoff is going to be and it's going to hurt.

Basically that's what I do and that's my philosophy.

USM: Can you say a little bit more about how parents are involved in an actual therapy session? Are they observers, or are they drawn in to participate more?

CJ: It really depends on how much heat and light there is between the child and the parents. Of the kids I have seen this week, I have seen all but one with their parents. I am choosing not to see that one child and we have never met. I just work with the parents. They're both case workers. They're involved in an open adoption, doing a fantastic job with the kid. Periodically they need to check in because something is getting unstable at home. But I'm not going to see their kid unless she starts showing some kind of pathology, and she's been getting better and better. She doesn't need to connect with somebody else she's going to lose.

The other kids I've seen with their parents. About half of them are in very healthy families where the issues are not family issues. They're issues with old families or with schools. Those parents mostly just sit quietly. They may add pieces of information. A kid may volunteer something and the parent will say, "That's why you were upset on Tuesday, and you know what you did when you were upset? What you did was 'X'." The kid had not made that connection. The parent will make that connection, but they do it in a very supportive way. They add to what's happening between the kid and me by giving us additional information. They become part of the therapy team.

The other half of the kids I've seen are at a war with their parents. If these people could do what they really wanted, they would annihilate each other. They are so angry because they are so hurt, rejected, misunderstood or devalued, that you bring them in here and you get this incredible white heat. Those people are going to yell and be mad and blame, and they're not going to talk for each other. They have to learn how to take time out and give themselves time to say things clearly, in a way that does not negate somebody else's feelings or thoughts, things they need to say to take care of the little kid inside them. And if they can do that one hour a week, I give homework. Everybody I see goes home with homework.

USM: Could you give us some examples?

CJ: If a family is in here because, if they're not, somebody's going to leave the family or hurt somebody, what they're doing is learning how to live together in a neutral enough environment that healing can begin. So we're diffusing by finding out, in this family's style of fighting, the rules that work, which are: "You are entitled to feel just as strongly as you need to feel, and you may hold on to your anger as hotly and strongly as you need to. Here's some things I can tell you to do with that anger that are not destructive to you or to anyone else in your family. I'm going to ask you to practice handling your anger in those ways, because the anger is causing distance in the family, and the distance is causing a lot of pain. We don't want you to hurt yourself or other people." That's homework.

Lots of times the kids or parents will suggest their own homework, in terms of what comes out of the session. One parent said this week, "I'm beginning to be aware that what's really happening in my family is not that Alexander is being overly angry or out of control, but that I never learned to be in a family where people were angry openly. In my family when people were angry they withdrew. So we need to figure out how I can deal with Alexander's anger, because when I listen to him talking about it, he has every right to be feeling what he's feeling, and I'm messing that up for him because it scares me." So I said to Alexander, "How do you think you can help your mom with that?", and Alexander said, "I think after I get mad I can give her a hug and tell her I love her." I said, "Okay, would that be hard for you to do?" He said, "Not at all. Sometimes I feel angry, but I always love her."

At this point, she is weeping because her fear of course is that when he's angry maybe he doesn't love her. In this family there has been a separation in the last three years, and the last male who got angry at her left. So that's a hot issue for her. She was able to own that, and then we talked about what she thought she needed to do. She said she needed to figure out that people had been getting angry at her, that she'd been trying to head that off and sending very mixed signals. And that she appreciated it, when she was doing this, that Alexander was strong enough to let her know it made him angry without leaving. She felt that she was leaving, by pulling back, going to her room, and bringing Alexander to a therapist to make him stop being angry. She thought about her life as we talked about it, and realized she really believed that anger was an appropriate thing; that when people were unjust, lied to you, betrayed you, or were hurting other people, you needed to bring forth that anger. She decided she doesn't want Alexander to stop being angry. She was going to figure out how he could safely be angry at her house, and how she could send him an unmixed message. When she said to him, "Alexander, it is all right to be angry," she could mean, "Even at me." She might need to come in and have some sessions on her own. Her homework was to think about knowing that he still loved her when he was angry and he was not going to leave; and, knowing now that she believed that anger was not just a one-sided, bad emotion, how she could tell him he was allowed to be angry so it wasn't scary for her. That's an example of homework. That just came out of the session; they assigned their own homework. Very often that's what happens. Sometimes I assign the homework. In another family I saw, the mother has gone back to work full-time. The father had a terrible childhood. They have an eleven-year-old who's running their family by being extraordinarily phobic, and they have a six-year-old that the eleven-year-old is babysitting every day after school until the parents get home. The eleven-year-old has enough going on that she really can't be very mindful of this little brother's feelings, and he's feeling totally abandoned. He's been trying to be a good sport and be brave, and not bother his sister because he knows some things are hard for her, and he's been trying to take care of everyone in his family when he's only six years old. His parents are sending him messages that six-year-olds don't have to take care of themselves. That's what happened to his dad, and his dad does not want that to happen to his son. So, he needs to reach out and how can he do that? The son said that it would help him if his parents would put a message on the tape recorder, so that when he came home from school one of his parents would have left a message saying, "Hi. How was your day? I'm thinking about you. If anything happens this afternoon, feel free to give me a call." So the homework was that the parents would be responsible for making sure there was a message on the tape for him to hear. He would be responsible for listening, and for reporting back to me whether that helped with his feeling lonely after school.

Also, the mother had said it bothered her that her son had been carrying this burden for five months, and she hadn't known. He had not told her, even when she asked. It made her very sad to know that he'd been doing that to take care of her, when what she really needs him to do to take of her is to tell her if something is hurting him, because her fear about going back to work is that something will not be good for him. So, his homework is to tell her how he feels about his day at school, so that when she comes home he won't have forgotten if something bothered him at school.

This week when he came in, I asked him to report on his homework, and he said it was really helping. He was angry that it was mostly his mom leaving the messages. He really needs to connect with his dad, because his dad is the one who knows what it feels like to be a six-year-old boy who feels you have to take care of everyone. His dad wants to connect with him, but really has no model to do that, and his dad said, "It's hard for me to talk to the tape recorder, but it's not hard for me to talk to you. But Mom calls you everyday to see how things are going, and you haven't been telling her. What if I call you?" And the kid said, "That might work, but what happens if you call me and it's not a time when my sister's being a jerk to me, and then later she is?" The dad said, "Well, then you call me," and he said, "I can't do that."

Then we explored why, and he's afraid that when he's upset he talks fast and people won't understand him. He can't ask for his dad by his real name. So we practiced. He could call and say his name and, "May I speak to my dad?" or "May I call and speak to Mr. So and So?" He said he thought he could do either of those, and his mother said, "Fine, tomorrow afternoon I'm not working, and we need to practice and I'll be there," at which point he burst into tears and said, "I'm never going to call either of you at work because it's too scary. I can't do it. Don't make me do it. It's too hard." Then we had to talk about why it was too hard, which he isn't clear on. So his homework was to figure out what the worst thing is that could happen, and we got some answers. One is that he could get the wrong number, because sometimes when he's upset he doesn't dial well, because he's only six. He can't ask his sister to dial if he's upset at her, because that's not a fair thing to ask her to do: "Call my parents so I can rat on you." He doesn't know what to do about the dialing. His parents reassured him that, at both businesses, the switchboard person would answer by saying the name of the business, and if he got a wrong number he just would have to hang up. He didn't have to talk to this person about having made a mistake. He said, "I still can't do it." His mother said, "You have to, and you have to do it when you're not upset so that you'll know what will happen."

So, the homework is that his parents are going to make him do something that I have said they must make him do. We all know it's going to be really hard, that he's going to feel like we are not listening to how hard and scary that is for him. We will help him any way we can. He has my phone number. They will call me if he needs to call me and tell me that I'm a real jerk, and I'm making him do something he hates, and its not fair because it's going to be a week between now and when I see him; I expect that he's going to call his dad every day this week, and I expect it's going to be really hard. That's another example of homework.

Another example is a kid who's in a behavior modification

classroom. He's throwing chairs. He's having temper tantrums seven or eight times, and he's really angry. He has wonderful parents. He's not having a problem at home, but he's having a terrible problem at school. His problem concerns control. He needs to be in charge, to be vigilant. He needs not to be surprised. When the teacher says, "Stop playing, and start working," he blows up. The school says this is because he doesn't want to work.

I said to him, "I don't think that's the problem at all. I think it's hard for you to hear 'Stop' and 'Start' because you've heard lots of stops and starts that hurt. What you're missing is something I think you can figure out." I drew a picture, and I put a red stop light on it, and he printed 'Stop' (he's practicing printing). I put a green light on it, and he printed 'Go'. I said, "What are we missing?" He said, "There's no yellow light." I said, "That's the problem. What does a yellow light say?" He said, "I don't know. What does a yellow light say?" I said, "A yellow light says slow down and be careful, and that's what you're missing." So then I put my hand in the middle of his belly and said, "All right, I want you to imagine that you are growing a yellow light." He closed his eyes tight and said, "I can feel it." I said, "Can you draw it?" "YES!" he said, and drew it. I said, "Now the secret is that when you start feeling like you're going to blow up, you can put your hand where the yellow light is and feel it, and you know what that will do? It will make you the boss of the time-out room," which you see he's printed at the top: "Danny is the boss of the time-out room." He said, "You mean all I have to do is use my yellow light and I can be in charge of whether or not I'm in the time-out room?" I said, "Danny, it's as easy as that." He said, "I can do that. That will work. Write this down for me. This is really important." So we wrote it down.

The parents said this helps at home too, and so they put a picture on their refrigerator at home. The mother's homework was to help him remember every day that he was growing a yellow light, and that it might not work every day, but that it would work some of the time, and the more he practiced it, the more aware he would be that he had it there to use.

The following week, I gave him a plastic bag of a dozen stop lights from a party favour store. They just had red and green lights and I said, "These remind me of you." He said, "We have to fix those, because now I have a yellow light. You know what I'm gonna do? I'm gonna take one of these to school and keep it

81

in my desk, and when I need it, I just have to hold on to it, and it will help me find my yellow light."

This is a kid who was blowing up seven to nine times a day at school; now he has blown three times in the last five weeks. Is that because I'm a magical therapist? No. It's because all you have to do is listen to kids, and they'll tell you what they're missing, what they don't know. That's learning error. To him it was either stop or start. He never had a chance to say, "Hey, wait, slow down, and let me have a say here." All I'm doing is giving him what he's needed all along, and its translating itself into the classroom. That's how you do homework.

USM: Would you describe yourself as influenced by behavioral theory, family therapy, or developmental ideas?

CJ: I am a child-taught therapist. The school where I did my graduate work is strongly developmental, and because that played itself so strongly in the kids lives that I'm seeing, I am colored by that. I stepped away from the developmental angle for a good period of time and became an expert on working with separation and loss issues in children, because all the kids I was seeing were working on those issues. That is my own work, because there was nobody to tell me. I had to invent it, by listening to what kids told me they needed. Now I have this whole body of ideas that I use that work. The kids told me they will tell anybody who will listen, so that's all you have to do, because they always tell you what they need. I do some TA, some behavior mod, some Gestalt, and a lot of pure intuition and inventiveness. I can't put a label on what I do; I hope there will never be a label. If I were to start doing one thing, then I would start seeing kids one way and stop listening to them. I don't want that ever to happen. There is no one way....

USM: You've referred to a number of kids graduating at this point with whom you have been working. Have you been seeing some of those kids for years?

CJ: No, I don't see people for years. The average length of time for me to work with a kid is around six months, unless there are real complications in the family. One youngster who went into an adoptive family was there for three years and was never finalized. I was called in to consult. The kid had tried to kill another kid. A decision needed to be made: was he safe, did he need to be contained, was he safe in a family, was he safe in this family? As a consultant, I see all of the adults involved and the kid once every five weeks. There is a therapist who sees the kid weekly. I do supervision with them, and everybody gets homework. The kid got remarkably well remarkably fast, which is one of the things that just happens for me. It isn't me; I don't want to take credit. I am extremely lucky, in a lot of ways. Very potent things happen here in a very short period of time.

Part of it is because I don't waste time. If there is something that we need to talk about, we talk about it right then, not wait until the next time. For example, Danny, the kid with the stop lights: I asked him to describe after a particularly bad day at school, how he was feeling before he blew up. And he said, "I really don't know. It happened so fast." Now, this kid, at age six, had told me that until he came into this family he didn't know he had feelings, and I think it's absolutely true. He had said, "I can tell you now what my feelings are, but did you know that until September I didn't know that I had feelings? But my mom and dad taught me I had feelings, so I know what they are." But here he said he didn't know how he was feeling. I said, "Can you tell me what you did, that was bad?" He said, "Well, I think I threw a chair, and I'm not sure about the others."

Now, this kid had been so straight with me. I wasn't sure whether he was in a total impulse rush with blackout, and I needed to know. After the session they went home. I called up the mom and said, "He may genuinely not remember, he may be having such an impulse rush that he doesn't know, and that's going to be making him feel very crazy." But then she said that she had asked him if he could tell her about the other bad things he did, and he told her exactly what happened. And she said to me, "It was the third time he had seen you, and I said to him, 'You haven't had any trouble telling Claudia anything. Why didn't you tell her?' and he said, 'Claudia is the first person who has ever understood me. I was afraid that she would get mad and not see me.'"

I said, "I want him to call me tonight," and he did. I said, "Danny, I have two very important things to say to you. I told you I would tell you what happened at the meeting" (because I told him I would report in. I always report in to kids, if I ever talk about a kid to anybody.) I said, "At the meeting people were absolutely full of smiles the entire time. They said you are doing incredible work, Danny. You still have rough days. We figured out some things we're going to try, so that we aren't setting you up to have rough days. The school thinks it can fix what is giving you the rough days. What I heard was that you're a fantastic kid, you're doing a fantastic job, the school wants to help you, and they think they can. We are working on a yellow light with them because they haven't been saying, 'Hey, wait a minute, Danny's going to need time about this one.'" Danny said, "Good, they need to do that."

I said, "But the thing I'm really worried about, and I really need you to help me on, is something your mother told me. She told me that you didn't tell me something, because you were afraid it would make me angry. What are the rules in the office?" He told me. I said, "What are the things that make me angry?" He said, "Breaking those rules." I said, "You're right. Is there any rule about anything you're not supposed to say?" He said no. I said, "I will promise you that there is nothing you could say in my office that will make me too angry to see you. I am making you a promise that I will never, ever, stop seeing you because I am angry. I am not making you a promise that I will not get angry at you, because I don't know how my feelings are going to go."

I called him that night, because I didn't want that to go to the next day. If you do that it saves enormous amounts of time, because then the kid doesn't have a whole week to build up fantasies. By the end of a week that kid could have thought he told me and I got angry and I didn't want to see him, because his reality hold is a little fuzzy. So I'm very straightforward.

One of the gifts I have been given over the last six years is that I have worked with a good number of resettled Cambodian minors. The majority of them are male. This poses a problem, because in an Asian culture, male/female relationships are very different than they are in this country. Most of these resettled young men are having control problems with their American mothers. And they're seeing an American-mother therapist. The gift they have given me is learning how to be assertive, straightforward, and confrontational without costing someone "face." They taught me a whole lot about Buddhism, about karma, about how to work with people who feel that they are not in control of their lives—their lives are in control instead. Most of the adolescents that I see feel that way, although they are not Asian. They've taught me about how you respect that belief and still empower someone. They've taught me about how to be straight with them without doing anything that invades someone's space or costs them "face."

I've worked as an adolescent therapist for 22 years, and I'm good at it. That is the only secret: you can't do anything that intrudes on their space; it costs them "face." If you can do that then the flow of health just bubbles through ... it's wonderful ... it's magic. Mostly what I do in here is exciting, it's empowering, for all of us. We share things very closely with each other. Magic takes place here, but the magic comes because, basically, in spite of what they act like and look like, the kids who come here have a glow of health, and all you have to do is put them in touch with it. All that takes is for you to believe that they've got it; the rest takes care of itself. Now, I don't know what you call that, but that's what it is, and it works.

USM: Let's turn to your consulting work. What is the mentor modeling you do?

CJ: One of the things that is exciting for me is that I am still seeing kids who are teaching me things. Because I'm getting harder and harder kids referred, I've done more training and had more interns, so there are a bunch of good people out there who know how to do what I do. They are now coming back and saying they can identify what they don't know. That's how the mentoring model started. I have people who have studied with me for two years who are in Maine, in Connecticut, in other places geographically. They aren't able to get supervision, and what they really need is not me to work their case, they don't need to make a referral; what they need is to figure out how to use what they know that they aren't *aware* that they know. The way it works is that somebody will call, sometimes a parent, often a therapist or social worker, who either knows somebody who interned with me or who has interned with me, and they say, "I've got a real problem in my case load. Will you consult?" and I say yes.

I did one last week with a kid who now is out of that family. It turned out that the real problem in the family, in addition to this kid's problem, is that the Dad had a significant problem none of us knew about. I wasn't involved in the placement. Ultimately the youngster needed to be moved. We worked on what kind of family we should be looking for, and on that subject, he drew a picture of himself and a dinosaur. I said, "What are you doing in the picture?" He said, "I'm digging up a dead dinosaur. I lived with that family and I got better, but it turned out there was a dead dinosaur in that family. And people kept saying to me it's your job to cover it up, and I couldn't cover it up, it was too big. I want a family like this, and when I dig up the dinosaurs (if there are any dinosaurs), I want them to say, 'Good, a dinosaur, let's have a dinosaur roast.'" That's really clear from an eight-year-old. That was a mentoring model kid. When in a nearby state doing training, I saw that kid for a total of three hours, in two one-and-one-half-hour segments.

I usually like to see the child at the end of one day, so I see what she or he is like after school when she or he is tired, and again at the beginning of the next day. Sometimes there is a real difference. That gives me some clues. I do some diagnostics that I've invented and some standard diagnostics, and then I sit down with all of the adults who are involved and say, "This is what came out in the diagnosis. This is what I think the kid's issues are. These are the things that I think we need to be treating. Now we need to decide who is most interested in doing what." And each person takes one thing off the list, and we agree that's the only thing that they are going to focus on. Then they stop feeling so overwhelmed. Most of the kids I see are pretty overwhelming, because they have so many things going on.

This child I mentioned who had tried to kill another child in school: that's overwhelming. And he was being very destructive at home, and running away, and he was not very old: he was seven. People were projecting what he was going to be like when he got to be an adult, and it was scary. Nobody wanted to be sued. He had been working with a therapist for eighteen months. Everybody was overwhelmed, so everybody picked one issue. The school psychologist said he would work on the school problems. The mother would work on nurturing, particularly the part that the kid never got, learning error. The father was going to work on anger issues. We talked about how they could do their work in their style, using how I work as a model. They had seen me work with the kid, because they all watched the diagnosis through a one-way mirror. The kid knew that they were on the other side.

Now I expect in a five-week period there's going to be a massive change in every single one of the areas. This kid had six people on his team, and I expect he would make five or six massive changes. When you're changing that fast, you have to be sure that you're not just changing symptoms, but what's underneath them. In five weeks people come back and say, "This worked, that didn't work, and now this is what we've got," so that we were sure we weren't just changing symptoms. Then we'd have another homework assignment.

About every three months I would see the kid, or more often if people felt that things were going on that they were confused about. They wanted me to check out whether this was progress, because sometimes progress in kids is hard to measure. You take a kid who won't speak to you, who is an elective mute, and the first thing that comes out of his mouth is usually pretty rotten; but you have to be able to see that as progress. Sometimes you are really not sure if it is, and you need somebody to say, "I'm not concerned about that at all" or, "Yes I think we should be concerned about that." My job is to be responsible for resolving any concern or impasse of the people who are doing the actual work. They are entitled to a phone call each week, for free, because I'm going to learn; they shouldn't have to pay for what they are teaching me, which is what they know that they aren't aware that they know. And that's been very exciting.

USM: Who are the members of the team you consult with?

CJ: Any of the adults who are involved with the problems the child is presenting. It may be a probation officer; it's almost always parents, unless the kid is in a residential treatment program. We may be talking about staff having problems; or about parents or visiting family. Today I'm consulting at Walker School in Needham, Massachusetts, and the family and kid probably won't be there because I'm not doing that kind of consulting model. I see the parents and kid every five weeks. Instead I'm working with the staff on how you work with some of these complicated issues. They are working on diagnosis and treatment implementation, developing a basic general philosophy about how to help kids go back home or move into adoption, that they can implement consistently throughout the house, school room, therapy sessions, with the family worker and with visits. They bring the whole staff together and try to be consistent, in terms of what they understand kids need.

They are also going to work on counter-transference issues, like "I don't want to be the one to say to this kid (you're not going home) because it's going to make me cry." Then we talk about why that hurts and whether it would hurt their relationship with the kid if they did cry: "If you really don't want to do it, who do you think is the logical person to do it?" Some of the things that they need to deal with at the Walker School are very difficult. They get a whole lot of support from each other, which is one of the reasons I'm willing to consult there. If I were a kid in big trouble and I needed to be in a place, to be taken care of, Walker is one of the places I would want to be. It's a wonderful treatment center.

Making an Impact: Post-Adoption Crisis Counseling
Lauren Frey

Introduction

In October 1986, Project IMPACT, Inc. of Boston, Massachusetts, began to offer intensive, in-home crisis intervention counseling as part of its post-adoption service program. The counseling is modeled after the Homebuilder program in Washington State, a therapeutic approach that has successfully prevented out-of-home placement for scores of children during the past twelve years (Kinney, et al. 1977). Project IMPACT, Inc. is currently using this four-week model of intervention with families who have legalized the adoption of an older, special-needs child and are subsequently facing the possibility of removing the child from their home, either because their child is choosing to leave or threatening to leave the home precipitously, or because the parents have decided that they can no longer parent this child in their home.

The Homebuilder model is a home-based mental health service designed to avoid the need to use substitute care for a child in any type of family. IMPACT is adding to this model its relevant knowledge of the developmental issues and dynamics of older-adopted special-needs children and their families. The agency is modifying the Homebuilder model to maximize its effectiveness in preserving permanent family ties for these children.

IMPACT has chosen to limit its present service to families who have adopted through IMPACT, its network agencies or the Massachusetts Department of Social Services. The need for this intensive service is indicated if there is an immediate or long-term risk of the adopted child leaving the home unless some changes occur. Families must live within one hour's traveling distance from Boston; and at least one parent must agree to participate in the intervention. At present, IMPACT can serve one family at a time in a four-week intervention. One-half of the full-time position of Post-Adoption Service Coordinator is devoted to providing this intensive counseling service.

The Crisis Model

In recent years, crisis intervention theory and practice has taken its place next to the other respected forms of brief therapy. Gerald Caplan, an important force in the development of crisis intervention, quoted in Aguilera and Messick (1974) defines a crisis as occurring "when a person faces an obstacle to important life goals that is, for a time, insurmountable through the utilization of customary methods of problem-solving".

Viewing crisis as an opportunity to alleviate stress, and as a motivator to learn new and more effective methods of coping, recent theorists have identified other important aspects of crisis intervention. Howard Parad maintains that the success of intervention was affected by timely response of the helper, intervening in a recently developed crisis where disequilibrium still existed. Central to this line of crisis intervention thinking was the role of the caseworker as an actively involved participant, observer and change agent (Golan 1978).

According to Lydia Rapoport, another dynamic force in the development of crisis theories and techniques, this type of practice necessitates that the social worker and client have quick and easy access to each other. Also of critical importance is the need for the therapeutic work to be present-oriented and geared toward the "restoration and enhancement of functioning" (Golan 1978).

Expanding upon current approaches to crisis intervention, the Homebuilder model combines five important aspects in forming this unique service. These aspects, outlined in "An Overview of the Homebuilder Program" (Kinney, et al, 1977), are summarized in the following paragraphs. IMPACT has used these Homebuilder principles to shape its own post-adoption crisis counseling service.

Families are reached while in crisis.

During a crisis, family members are more open to learning alternate ways of responding and coping, in order to relieve their present pain. A crisis is an opportunity for growth. Being available to a family during an extremely stressful time often helps in developing a trusting and positive relationship between the family and social worker.

Counseling takes place at home.

Meeting with family members on their home turf has many advantages. It is usually more convenient and comfortable for the families, and the social worker is able to develop a much more realistic and holistic assessment of the situation. This aspect of the model places the social worker in the midst of family life, enabling timely interventions to be made and allowing these interventions to be evaluated and changed, if necessary.

Help is never far away.

The social worker is on-call to the family 24 hours a day, seven days a week, during the four- to six-week counseling period. The social worker makes a commitment to respect the family's daily routine and meet their scheduling needs. A social worker is able to visit whenever requested by the family, to stay as long as necessary, and to return as soon as the family requests it. Supervisors are able to make planned visits and remain on call to a family during the temporary absence of a social worker.

Counseling is flexible.

Social workers are trained to use techniques from behavior modification, Thomas Gordon's Parent Effectiveness Training, Rational Emotive Therapy, Carl Roger's client-centered therapy, and assertiveness training, as well as their own personal counseling style and experience. They are trained to help the families formulate their own goals for counseling, and they help each family to design a creative treatment plan that is in tune with the family's values, abilities and needs. Some services that social workers might provide are: intervening in crises; providing advocacy with legal, medical or educational systems; teaching behavior management, negotiation, communication or assertiveness skills; and locating food, shelter, transportation, health care, respite care or financial assistance.

Counseling is carefully documented and evaluated.

For maximum progress tailored to a family's needs, the counseling is based on behaviorally-specific goals and evaluated by goal attainment scaling. This allows for interventions to be changed if progress is not occurring. This aspect of the model also helps to demystify the counseling process, allowing family members to own their progress, acknowledging their inner strengths and abilities to change.

Post-Adoption Interventions: Project IMPACT's Experience
During the first eight months of IMPACT's post-adoption crisis counseling service, five families requested and participated in an intervention. One additional family participated in an intake session, and then decided that they wanted to try to make some changes on their own before pursuing an intensive counseling service. Two other families requested or were referred for intervention, but could not be served within the parameters of the program. One of these families had adopted through a non-IMPACT, private agency and the other family lived in western Massachusetts, a traveling distance of three hours from Boston. Most recently, one family requested that their intervention begin as soon as they could terminate the stay of their daughter in a psychiatric hospital.

The following paragraphs describe four adoptive families who participated in interventions. The services they sought, why they sought them, their most important goals, and the outcomes of the interventions are all discussed.

Family Y
The Y family sought post-adoption resources from IMPACT at a point when the mother, a single parent of two girls aged 9 and 14, had become overwhelmed by several significant stresses in her life. The oldest daughter had begun behaving aggressively toward her mother and exhibiting an increase in non-compliant behavior. Ms. Y first requested extended respite care, and negotiated a one-month stay for her oldest daughter with an experienced foster and adoptive family in the IMPACT network. At the end of that month, Ms. Y requested an intensive four-week intervention as she looked toward reintegrating her daughter into the home. Other stresses impinging upon this family were the recent death of Ms. Y's mother, the recent pre-adoptive placement of the youngest girl into the Y home, and the decision to have Ms. Y's friend and young daughter move into the home while going through a divorce.

The two goals chosen by this family were: increasing the oldest daughter's compliant behavior concerning household chores and rules; and increasing the mother's ability to alleviate her own stress and to take care of herself emotionally. Very early in the intervention, Ms. Y chose to disrupt the placement of the youngest daughter, as one way to relieve some of her own stress and to concentrate her efforts upon her oldest daughter.

Several themes emerged during this intervention (extended to five weeks at Ms. Y's request) that may have affected the outcome significantly. Ms. Y struggled a great deal to gain realistic expectations of herself as an adoptive parent of an emotionally troubled child, and reasonable expectations for her daughter regarding attachment and family loyalty. Particularly unsettling to this daughter was her mother's threat that this month represented their "last try to make it work." The respite care family's need to "rescue" rather than provide relief was extremely unhelpful to Ms. Y and her daughter.

A few weeks after the end of IMPACT's intervention, the daughter left Ms. Y to live with the respite care family, and Ms. Y attempted to surrender her back into state care. The respite family has since been granted temporary guardianship through the court. In a follow-up evaluation, Ms. Y commented that she had hoped this counseling might "help (her daughter) see and understand better what a family was all about."

Family S

The S family, a single mother with two daughters, requested a shorter IMPACT intervention, feeling that removal from the home was not imminent, but that if the problems continued, there was a risk that the adopted daughter might run away.

Ms. S had one biological daughter, aged 14, and one adopted daughter, aged 15, who came to her home ten years ago as a foster child. During this intensive, three-day intervention, Ms. S wanted help with understanding and living with her daughter's conflicting family loyalties, decreasing her daughter's extreme temper outbursts, and engaging her daughter in ongoing therapy.

A major theme became the adopted daughter's difficulty discriminating between public and private information, what should and should not be shared with people outside of one's family. She said that her own life had been "an open book." All the details of her life "were in a case record for everyone to read." She did not value privacy as did her adoptive family. Also a constant source of frustration for Ms. S was that her daughter reacted to any family conflict by "recruiting" a new family for herself. As Ms. S said, "Her way to solve every problem is to find someone else to live with."

This daughter continues to live at home, and has continued in individual therapy, to which she contributes financially. In their follow-up evaluation, this family reported that the daughter had more control of her tantrums, and that the mother had gained some valuable adoption-related information.

Family H

The H family includes a single parent and her three children; one biological son, aged 15, one adopted son, aged 17, and one adopted daughter, aged 8. Ms. H called IMPACT because her adopted son, who is severely learning-disabled and quite vulnerable in the community, had run away a few weeks earlier, but returned the next day. Ms. H hoped that IMPACT could help her understand the recent increase in her adopted son's troubling behaviors, which included running away, angry and aggressive outbursts, particularly toward his younger sister, and non-compliance with household chores.

This family also chose a three-day intervention. In addition to giving this son an opportunity to learn new ways to manage his anger, there were two other important focal points of the counseling. One was helping mother and sons to communicate more openly with each other; and the other to encourage and support this mother in the very difficult task of parenting her adopted son. His neurological impairments, combined with his early life experiences and adolescent development, presented a complex situation for him and his family. He had few social outlets or ways to gain competence and self-confidence outside of the family, and his quest for independence and control of his own life will most likely continue to frustrate him and worry his mother. He continues to live at home since IMPACT's intervention.

Family L

The L family consisted of a single parent and her twelve-year-old adopted daughter. Ms. L called IMPACT "because something has to change and I don't know where else to turn." She reported that her daughter had recently begun skipping school, stealing, breaking curfew rules, physically striking out at her mother, having serious tantrums, breaking possessions, destroying property and locking herself in the bathroom.

Ms. L was considering psychiatric hospitalization for her daughter but was hoping to avoid it. She commented that she was not "ready to give up, but almost." This mother hoped to gain even a small indication that her daughter cared about the future of this family and to increase the daughter's ability to hold a conversation with her mother without screaming or having an outburst of temper.

A primary goal was to teach negotiation skills that would help the daughter "get more of what she wanted" and help the mother experience more success in parenting this child. A goal that was not initially stated but quickly became a priority was to plan ways to defuse the intensity of mother-daughter interactions and ways to help this mother manage the high level of crisis precipitated by her daughter daily. Regular respite care became a critical support to this mother, as did having an "on-call" social worker who would respond when needed.

Although direct intervention and skill-teaching with the daughter seemed to have little effect, Ms. L insisted that she, herself, benefited a great deal from the learning and support. She found universalizing her adoption experience a comfort. Her hope of getting services without dissolving the adoption was crucial.

Ms. L chose to hospitalize her daughter three months after the intervention. She saw this as her only option, given the level of danger and potentially self-injurious behavior that her daughter continued to exhibit. Ms. L. is actively involved in the hospital's evaluation process and in making thoughtful and realistic decisions about her child's future. Of great significance was Ms. L's comment that, most importantly, IMPACT's crisis intervention service helped her to "continue being a mother."

One modification of the Homebuilder model quickly emerged while working with these adoptive families. At the families' requests, a three-day intervention was offered instead of the usual four-week one. This was designed not as an assessment tool as in the Homebuilder model, but as a treatment option. A timely response to each family's request for service was important, and a very brief intensive intervention was better suited to the needs of some. This approach was used quite successfully by families to open lines of communication; to review birth family information and placement histories; to restate their commitment to the adopted child; to reflect on the child's growth in the family; and to gather new strength and resources. The three-day intervention enabled some families to move ahead on their own without further intensive service.

A theme that was prominent in all interventions with adoptive families was that of family loyalty. All the adopted children were struggling with birth family fantasies and high degrees of ambivalence about their current family relationships. Almost all of their troubling behaviors seemed connected to conflicts with identity, searching, belonging, and intimacy. The continuing challenge for these adoptive parents was in creatively parenting their adopted child, and maintaining a flexible perception of "family." In relation to the family loyalty issue, challenges emerge not only for the adoptive parents, but also for the helping professionals and the wider service system. The social worker must be able to assess accurately the adopted child's conflict about family loyalties and fears of belonging, and put it into perspective. In most every case, this child's best chance to cope with these inner conflicts and to develop healthy interpersonal relationships in the future lies in maintaining ties with his or her adoptive family. This means that the helping professional and service system must be prepared to design and respect nontraditional living arrangements for some of these families. Getting help to sustain the positive aspects of their family relationships may be a more realistic goal for some adoptive families than remaining under the same roof.

Another unifying theme was a universal request for concrete services and on-going support. Respite care and family therapists with an understanding of adoption were requested most often. Financial help with these services was also needed by two families. All of the families wanted to be connected to follow-up services after the intervention.

IMPACT's post-adoption crisis intervention service is still very new. The families who have participated report that it was worthwhile and helpful. These families have also predicted that because of the cyclical nature of crisis within adoptive families, they may need to access the service more often. Working with adoptive families may teach us that their success must be defined differently than the way it is defined within the Homebuilder model. IMPACT is continuing to offer this service and listen to the adoptive families' evaluations. The real experts have always been the families, and they will go on teaching us.

The Intrusive Therapies
Foster Cline

Frequently, adopted and foster children have disturbed early life histories characterized by pain, abandonment, abuse, neglect or frequent moves. Such children are often resistant to traditional therapeutic methods. *Traditional methods build a therapeutic relationship based on the presence of basic trust.* Basic trust is implanted within the first year of a child's life and if absent, most traditional methods of therapy have been ineffective, as the child is unable to form a "therapeutic relationship" or develop a "positive transference" or "working alliance."

Intrusive techniques, on the other hand, do not assume the presence of basic trust, but form it in various ways by purposely recapitulating the first year of life experiences.

The intrusive techniques include, but are not limited to, the following methods: holding therapy; rage reduction therapy; purposeful containment; intrusive high confrontation; time-limited scoldings; physical methods such as electric prods; and placement in highly demanding and forceful outdoor "awareness programs." With adults, intrusive techniques are used in reality attack groups and in certain drug or substance abuse rehabilitation centers.

Intrusive techniques have been "toyed with" reluctantly or enthusiastically for many years. All of these techniques have had their strong adherents, often fairly charismatic individuals who, when using the treatment, appear to have astonishingly quick results with very difficult individuals. Often the intrusive techniques are shunned by the professional community, and frustrated parents "go to bat" for a beleaguered professional who has successfully reached their children by strong, non-traditional techniques. The professionals and non-professionals who do express qualms are often fired by honest disagreement, sometimes by a lack of knowledge and perhaps sometimes even by professional jealousy. Detractors doubt the wisdom of intrusive techniques and make such assessments as, "That doesn't always work," "That can be harmful!," "I wouldn't want something like that done to me!," or "In the wrong hands that could be disastrous!"

Those advocating intrusive techniques generally agree with the above concerns, but feel that when attempting to reach severely disturbed and unbonded children, a thoughtful risk is worth possible misunderstanding by the professional community and the risk of legal entanglements.

Intrusive techniques all have a number of independent, or at times interdependent, goals. They attempt to:

- Force attention

- Force interaction

- Force acceptance of the therapist's reality

- Force compliance

- Force responsiveness and a reciprocal loving response

Although the word "force" could be euphemistically replaced with "encourage" or "promote" in the list above, let's call it what it is and settle for the use of the word "force" when referring to intrusive techniques.

Loving, kindness and tenderness are essential elements of intrusive techniques. This is often lost on those who are not completely familiar with them. The "capitulation," sobbing and snuggling that follow the rage induced by an intrusive technique are encouraged by an expressive and loving therapist.

Indications for Intrusive Techniques

1. Contract for the therapy is always attempted with individuals of all ages and is certainly expected when using such therapy with adults or older children.

2. Intrusive techniques should not be considered unless other more traditional methods have been attempted without positive results by a competent therapist.

3. The client has a history of infantile or toddler problems, and shows the results of such problems, specifically:

- Self-abuse

- Cruelty to animals

- Lack of affection toward primary care takers

- Superficial friendliness to strangers

- Speech problems
- Thought disorders—specifically with cause-and-effect thinking
- Problems with food
- Severe control battles at home and usually at school

The Theory of Intrusive Techniques

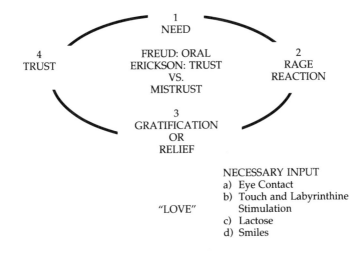

First Year of Life Cycle

The above cycle is the cycle of basic trust or bonding that takes place during the first year. It is important. The cycle turns thousands of times over the months, every time an infant is fed. This cycle starts with a need, followed by a rage reaction. Others have called this the tension-relaxation cycle. In infancy, the need is natural and the rage naturally follows. Intrusive techniques purposefully induce the rage, in essence to kick the cycle into spinning. The rage is easily accessible in some younger children who have trouble with loving contact, who are defensive toward touch, and in whom simple holding leads to bonding and attachment. Intrusive techniques, when used with such children, are not particularly controversial. The process can be diagrammed as:

> Child is
> > active
> > unresponsive
> > defensive to touch
> > out of control

Child is held → tension
↓
rage → relaxation
↓
capitulation
↓
sobbing + snuggling
↓ → loving acceptance by therapist
bonding

Working with older children is not so simple or non-controversial. Often older latency-age children refuse to form loving or bonding relationships, but their anger is less accessible and "tapped" by their more intact ego defense mechanisms. The rage inherent in such children is less accessible, because the child refuses to resist and passively (but without an attachment response) accepts holding and "goes limp." Such children need to be "intruded upon" more to break through their control mechanisms. *In all such cases it is essential for the therapist to make certain the child's resistance is not an appropriate response to an overcontrolling or unresponsive home environment.* If such children are treated with intrusive techniques, they will not be helped at best, and will become resentful and more controlling at worst. The therapist must make sure that the parents know correct parenting techniques before the therapist uses intrusive techniques.

This situation is diagrammed as:

```
┌─────────────────────────────────┐
│  Child is                       │
│      unresponsive to requests   │
│      controlling                │
│      sneaky                     │
│                                 │
└─────────────────────────────────┘
```

This child is held
↓
Child's response: "OK, hold me and now what?!—I'll lay here for hours ... you can't make me mad."
↓
Psychological and physical provocation by therapist
↓
Tension
↓
Feeling of helplessness in child
↓
Child expresses anger
↓
Encouragement & acceptance of anger by therapist
↓
Relaxation
↓
Stronger intrusive push by therapist
↓ → Tension
Rage
↓
Relaxation
↓
Capitulation with sobbing and snuggling
↓
Loving response by therapist
↓
Bonding

In summary, the intrusive techniques have many disadvantages:

1. They can be misused.

2. They do not come naturally to loving souls.

3. They must be taught through example and careful tutoring.

4. They may escalate control battles.

5. They may be completely misunderstood by other professionals in the community.

6. They present difficult legal ramifications.

7. They are often not helpful with run-of-the-mill neurotics (conflicted souls who live a life of woe and agony as a lifestyle).

However, offsetting these many disadvantages, intrusive therapy has one marked advantage: it is the best, quickest and perhaps only way of purposefully reaching unbonded children, character-disturbed individuals or neurotics who hide life-threatening conflicts and self-destructiveness behind massive denial.

Kim—The Case for Intrusive Therapy

Kim, adopted at six months, never formed a loving or responsive relationship with either of her parents. One older sister, also adopted (at birth) did well. Parents demonstrated excellent parenting techniques, but found Kim uncontrollable. At age 13, Kim was hositalized for one year at a metropolitan psychiatric hospital. In the hospital, her frequent rages led to restraint. After discharge from the hospital, through her mid-teens, Kim had difficulty in school, toyed with substance abuse, was sexually active with underachieving boys, and continued to refuse any kind of parental limits. After years of traditional therapy and hospitalization, the parents were "at a complete loss."

When I first saw Kim at age 16, she was dropping out of high school, had completed two abortions, and showed periods of reactive and uncontrollable rage toward her parents that were occasionally followed by periods of brief remorse and suicidal ideation.

Kim admitted to having a great deal of rage but noted, "I don't have any today." I explained to Kim that I would treat her according to her emotional age, regardless of her physical age, and she agreed that when in a rage, she acted like a two-year old. I told her that if she showed two-year-old rage I would hold her in my lap. Her response was, "Well, that will be interesting..." The second session was uneventful and Kim "passed time", and I dismissed her from the therapeutic hour stating that she was quietly fooling herself and needed to get in touch with some deeper feelings. The next session she entered, after a day of physical fighting with her parents, and paced up and down my office yelling, "Well, if you wanted to see me f___ing angry, I'm f___ing angry now!"

I quickly put Kim on my lap and held her, and she immediately went into a rage, followed by sobbing and snuggling and an admission that she had fouled up everyone's life, most of all her own. I brought in her father from the waiting room, and with my instructions he held her, and Kim went through fifteen solid minutes of rage, with her father, with eye-to-eye contact.

One month later, Kim noted, "I sure have a lot better relationship with my folks. I think I'm more content. Yeah, that's a good word, 'content'." Following the rage session, Kim was open to the usual type of therapy and her feelings were easily accessible and could be handled with traditional techniques.

IV. Educational and Social Support Groups and Events

An Overview
Karen Tilbor

Ideally, educational services to adoptive parents should begin before the child is placed. Accurate information, whether it pertains to the potential impact of adoption issues on normal stages of child development or to issues such as child sex abuse and attachment, can assist parents in understanding their adopted child's history and behavior. The group process utilized by special-needs adoption agencies provides a model for pre-placement education of all adoptive parents. Some agencies and expert consultants also offer workshops for adoptive parents on subjects that may have special relevance as a child reaches specific stages of development. Examples of such workshop topics are:

- Child development
- Parenting techniques
- Discipline
- Telling your child about adoption
- Recognizing and dealing with loss
- Infertility and sexuality
- Adolescent identity

- Sexual abuse

- Search process

The group experience offers the added benefit of adoptive parents becoming acquainted and supporting one another. But when groups are not available, educational opportunities can be structured individually by adoption and mental health professionals in various settings. Education and therapy may also be provided concurrently to meet a family's needs. As Foster Cline, elsewhere in this book, advises, "Therapy should not be done with a family when education will suffice."

The importance of social support, which seems obvious for any family, has a special significance in the life of an adoptive family. The adoptive family can't always count on the level of family and community support that generally surrounds a family preparing for biological children. *In Raising Adopted Children*, Lois Melina (1986) describes some of the special circumstances of adoptive parents:

> Becoming parents in a way different from the norm can help prepare people for future adjustments, but can also be confusing. Sociologist H. David Kirk, in his books *Shared Fate* and *Adoptive Kinship*, says that when there is a contradiction between the way people have been culturally prepared for an expected event—such as parenthood—and the way it really happens, people experience a "role handicap." As adoptive parents, we experience a role handicap not only because we expected to become parents in a different way, but because our culture does not provide support for alternatives to becoming a parent other than through birth. We must adapt birth announcements to our circumstances, try to get our employers to make exceptions to the companies' maternity leave policies.

Whether or not an adoptive family anticipates or experiences difficulties, they can reduce the sense of isolation by developing a functional support system, including other adoptive families when possible. The task of fostering both a sense of belonging in the child and an acceptance of how adoption is different from other ways of joining a family can be eased by interacting with people in similar situations. Families that have developed a strong support system are more likely to reach out for professional help when they need it. When such a support system is not in place, the job of the professional becomes greater.

One responsibility of the professional is to help the family create a dependable support system where one does not exist. If this is not done, the family may become too dependent upon professional support or, lacking that connection, continue to struggle while problems persist or accelerate.

Services developed by several special-needs adoption agencies demonstrate their understanding of the basic need for social support. Parent support groups and buddy families are among the supportive structures built into some programs, such as that of Family Resources in New York. In the videotape, which accompanies this book, *Adoption—A Lifelong Process* (Tilbor, Coleman, et al., 1987), Joan McNamara of Family Resources in New York notes: "We have a camping weekend for families and the emphasis is on the tennis courts…. But we also have workshops for parents and kids, and one of the things we do there is a joint workshop with teens and parents, and connect things that have gone on over the weekend in the various workshops." Family Resources nurtures an environment that allows things to happen. McNamara continues: "If someone's willing to connect, for example, with a Buddy Family, they are much more likely—after adoption when a problem arises—to reach out to that Buddy Family again. If they are unable to make those connections then, they have nowhere to turn."

Several agencies sponsor special events that they encourage adoptive families they have served to attend. The annual and bi-annual weekend events—such as family camping programs sponsored by Maine Adoption Placement Service and Family Resources, and Project Impact's residential weekend on a Boston college campus—are well-attended and become the source of stories and memories over the years. Some integrate educational programs for parents with the obvious social benefits of families sharing meals and recreation. And children get to know and share experiences with peers who are adopted, and of the same race or culture.

While most social support groups and events were initiated to support older child adoptions, the concept has been expanded to include other adoptive groups. Increasingly, parents of infants and toddlers, many of whom are bi-racial or from foreign cultures, are organizing to meet on a regular basis. The possibilities are limitless, but activities generally focus on pot-luck suppers, picnics, lectures, and family-oriented cultural events. The degree of social and educational emphasis can vary to suit each group, while the opportunity for mutual support continues.

The Search
Loren Coleman

Agencies and individuals concerned with adoption frequently create informal gatherings and events that can have a therapeutic impact on older adoptees. The production of these groups and happenings often issue from a specific problem or need, but sometimes are developed merely to fill a void of social linkages felt by adoptive families.

In recent years there has been an explosion of interest and involvement in nonprofessionally led groups concerning one specific issue: the search for biological families. For adoptees reaching adolescence, seeking a sense of self is an important milestone. Joan McNamara sees the questioning of identity most teenagers exhibit as quite healthy. She writes in *The Adoption Advisor* that these questions are inevitable, and feels the "need to know about parents and grandparents or racial or national origins comes up in every family. The teenager tries to come to some resolution with all the diverse factors that brought him to where he now stands" (McNamara 1975: 159). She suggests, as do many others, such as the Klibanoffs in *Let's Talk About Adoption* (1973), that the adoptive parents should help the adoptee in search of roots as a demonstration of love.

Three women have made special contributions to the acceptance of searching by adoptees, and their influence is far-reaching. Over thirty years ago, an adopted social worker, Jean M. Paton, searched for and found her mother when she was 47 and her mother was 69. Paton founded Orphan Voyage of Cedar Edge, Colorado, as a program of mutual aid and guidance for adults searching for their birthparents or relatives. Paton had written and lectured widely on the topic of adoption, and her book *Orphan Voyage* (1968) describes her search and others. She believes, in the eyes of our culture, adoptees never reach full adult status and are always seen as "adopted children." She advocates the "reunion file" as a way of maintaining and updating information on the adoptees and their biological parents. When the adoptee reaches adulthood, either party could use the file to initiate a contact, if both parties agree.

Florence Ladden Fisher is the founder of ALMA, the Adoptees Liberty Movement Association, which advocates the removal of barriers—legal, social and agency—that prevent adult adoptees from discovering their biological heritages. ALMA is becoming more widespread from its origins in Fisher's New York, and is now operating through branches across the nation. Fisher views the sealed records as an affront to human dignity, and holds the adoptee's need to know his or her hereditary background as a necessary part of identity formation. She believes a closer relationship with the adoptive family may be one of the outcomes of finding one's birthparents, and adoptive parents should not view the searching as rejection.

Fisher spent a determined twenty years in searching for her own parents. Of all the early search books, hers was among the most popular, well-read, and publicized. *The Search for Anna Fisher* (1973) is an emotion-packed, detailed opus which pulls the reader along through heartbreaking confrontations with the wall of people guarding adoption "secrets."

Fisher vividly describes many issues—for example, how she was made to feel everything "bad" was based on biology and her heritage, but everything "good" was a product of the adoptive home. Such items stirred up doubts inside her and left her with many unanswered questions. Her own identity crisis resolved itself with her reunion with her birthmother, and later with her birthfather. Today, she has a tenuous relationship with her mother and a very close one with her father.

The third woman to chronicle the experiences she had in searching for her birthparents is Betty Jean Lifton. Her books *Twice Born: Memoirs of an Adopted Daughter* (1975), *Lost and Found* (1979), and *I'm Still Me* (1981) introduced Lifton to her readers as an intelligent and emotional writer.

Lifton was adopted when she was two-and-a-half years old. When she was seven, her mother told her a "secret" she could not even tell her adoptive father—that she was adopted. Growing up believing both her birthparents were dead, it was not until she was thirty that she began her search, that ended with finding her birthmother.

Betty Jean Lifton's marriage to an empathetic and supportive psychiatrist added his fire to the movement. Robert Jay Lifton's impassioned foreword in Benet's *The Politics of Adoption* (1976) calls for a professional reexamination of cliches about the motivation of the search as neurotic dissatisfaction or unresolved Oedipus complex. Indeed, Betty Jean Lifton comments in *Twice Born* (1975):

> I used to say that if Freud had been adopted, everything would be different, for he would have understood that the Oedipus myth* was really about an adoptee's search; now I decided that if Freud had been married to an adoptee, it would have been just as good.

Betty Jean Lifton, Jean Paton and Florence Fisher are in the forefront of the adoptee search movement, and the byproducts have been organizations other than ALMA and Orphan Voyage. In 1975, Lifton referenced several: Detroit's Adoption Identity Movement, Chicago's Yesterday's Children, Washington's Adoptees in Search, Philadelphia's Adoption Forum, Denver's Search, and the Twin Cities, Minnesota's LINK. Today the American Adoption Congress headquartered in Washington, D.C., serves as the umbrella organization of a nationwide collection of sixty-six such groups. Regional organizations have increased dramatically; by 1984, Illinois, for example, had thirteen local groups spread throughout the state (Beckstead and Kozub, 1984). These groups can best be discovered by reviewing the publications or referral information from Independent Search Consultants, Inc., P.O. Box 10857, Costa Mesa, CA 92627. Their access to books and other data on the subject of search is extensive.

In 1976, another dynamic woman and groundbreaker in the adoption reform movement, Lee Campbell, joined with other birthparents in forming the first group for another corner of the adoption triangle. This national group, Concerned United Birthparents (CUB), now based in Des Moines, Iowa, is composed of biological parents, and is interested in a freer exchange of information. CUB sponsors chapters or informal groups that involve adoptees (Campbell, 1979). Teenage members can express internal conflicts and confusion before they initiate a full-scale search after reaching the age of majority (Anderson, 1987). Jon Ryan's National Organization for Birthfathers and Adoption Reform (NOBAR, P.O. Box 1553, Rochester, NH 03867) is a late 1980s product of the continuing adoption reform

---

* "Do you know who your parents are?"— Sophocles, *Oedipus Rex*

movement, and the new birthfather support and resource network. NOBAR is open to anyone whose life has been or may be affected by adoption.

Recent years have seen the institutionalize of the search as "a professional casework service" (Auth and Zaret, 1986). The studies and literature on the subject have increased dramatically (see especially, Sorosky, Baran and Pannor, 1978; and Triseliotes, 1980). The recognition of the need to support adoptive families, adoptees, and birthparents through the process of the search is a relatively new phenomenon. As Auth and Zaret (1986:567) note:

> The request for search is normal; every person who has been adopted speculates at one time or another about his or her birthparents. Most adoptees, either as children or adults, would like to meet their birthparents...
>
> Even though search states a goal to be achieved, it is a process with many stages. It often serves as a developmental task that must be worked on over a long period.

Because of the nature of the search—to date a process primarily occurring outside of the legal framework of adoption social services—support through informal channels is often the only option available to members of the adoption triad. Professionals working in the adoption field, therefore, would be advised to avail themselves of this informal network and referral system in their supportive post-adoption work.

About the Editors
and the Authors

Loren Coleman, M.S.W., Simmons College, B.A., Southern Illinois University, maintains a private clinical and consultation practice in Portland, Maine, and is a Research Associate at the Human Services Development Institute, University of Southern Maine. Mr. Coleman has been the Project Director of USM's two most recently federally funded adoption grants. He has been working with adolescents and their families for over two decades, and has been involved with adoption issues affecting birthparents, adoptees and adoptive parents since 1972. Mr. Coleman is the author or coauthor of *Suicide Clusters* (Faber and Faber, 1987), *Unattended Children* (USM, 1987), and *Gay and Lesbian Foster Parents* (USM, 1988); and is producer/director of the videos, *SOS - Teen Suicides and Runaways: Coded Cries for Help* (USM 1986) and *Adoption - A Lifelong Process* (USM 1987). In addition to his human services work, Mr. Coleman is an internationally known researcher and writer on cryptozoological topics, having authored four nonfiction books on the subject.

Karen Tilbor, M.S. Ed., Wheelock College, is a Research Assistant at the Human Services Development Institute. She has been field coordinator for the training and demonstration project on Mental Health Services of Older Adopted Children, Executive Producer of the videotape, *Adoption - A Lifelong Process* (1987) and coordinator of the second state-wide conference on child sexual abuse at Bethel, Maine. Her current projects include organizing state-wide training for child welfare supervisors in Maine and helping develop services pertaining to adoption of older children in three states. Her background in teaching and educational administration includes $4^1/2$ years as Education Director of a pre-school and after-school day care program in New York City.

Helaine Hornby, M.A., University of Southern Maine, is Director both of HSDI's Child and Family Policy Unit and the

National Child Welfare Resource Center for Administration and Management, which conducts research and provides technical assistance to states on child welfare policy and management. Ms. Hornby has directed numerous state and federally funded research and technical assistance projects in child welfare. She is co-author of *Learning from Adoption Disruption Insights for Practice* (USM, 1986) and author of "Why Adoptions Disrupt and What Agencies Can Do To Prevent It," *Children Today*, July-August 1986.

Carol Boggis, M.S., Colorado State University, is a consulting editor, audiovisual specialist and owner of *cjb productions* in Portland, Maine. She has edited numerous publications by HSDI and other human service agencies on such topics as adoption disruption, adolescent suicide prevention, unattended children, and elderly home care. Ms. Boggis has also authored many technical and popular articles and conference papers.

Jean-Pierre Bourguignon, Ph.D., Montreal University, is the founding director of Consultants in Developmental Behavioral Dysfunction in Evanston, Illinois, an agency dealing exclusively with families and children in all stages of adoption. A native of Belgium, he has extensive professional and academic credits in pediatric neuropsychology and behavioral medicine. Dr. Bourguignon has lectured extensively about foster care and adoptive placements both in the United States and abroad. In 1984 he received the "Friend of Children" award of the Ninth North American Conference on Adoptable Children, in recognition of his work with children and adoptive families.

Foster W. Cline, M.D., University of Colorado, is in private practice in Evergreen, Colorado. He completed his surgical and medical internship in the Panama Canal Zone and Adult and Child Psychiatric Residency at the University of Washington in 1971. Dr. Cline founded Evergreen Consultants, a multi-disciplinary clinic where children and families from throughout the world have come for intensive treatment. In the past three years, Dr. Cline has presented over 400 seminars to school systems, psychiatric treatment centers, and professional organizations, across the United States and five foreign countries. He has authored numerous books and videotaped materials that are available through Evergreen Consultants (P.O. Box 2380, Evergreen, CO 80439) or the Cline/Fay Institute (P.O. Box 2362, Evergreen, CO 80439). Dr. Cline has four children, one an older adoptee, and has foster-parented three other children.

Lauren Frey, M.S.W., is Post-Adoption Service Coordinator at Project IMPACT, Inc., an adoption agency for older, special-needs children in Boston, Massachusetts. Ms. Frey provides intensive, home-based crisis intervention services to families who have legally adopted children or teenagers through IMPACT, its network agencies, or the Massachusetts Department of Social Services. Ms. Frey has had ten years of experience in the human services field and seven years in adoption. She recently served as intern at the Homebuilders program in Federal Way, Washington, where she was trained in an intensive model of crisis intervention and family education. Ms. Frey has adapted this training to meet the particular needs and issues facing adoptive families.

Claudia L. Jewett, M.A., Tufts and Goodard Colleges, has worked as a child and family therapist in private practice for the past 22 years. She has served on the boards of the Open Door Society of Massachusetts, the Northeast Region Adoption Council, the Massachusetts Adoption Resource Exchange, the North American Council on Adoptable Children, and the North American Center on Adoption of the Child Welfare League of America. She is author of *Helping Children Cope with Separation and Loss* (Harvard Common Press, 1982) and *Adopting the Older Child* (same, 1978), a chapter on adolescents in *Adoption, Current Issues and Trends* (Butterworth, Canada, 1984), and other works. Ms. Jewett has provided case consultation or supervision for many agencies and has presented training for caseworkers, therapists and parents across the U. S. and Canada. She has taught courses at 40 universities and colleges. She was keynote speaker at the 1982 International Congress on Adoption and the 1986 meeting of the National Foster Care Association of Great Britain, where she conducted training sessions. Ms. Jewett has 10 children, 7 of whom were older adoptees.

Sharon Kaplan, M.S., has been Director of Parenting Resources, Tustin, California since 1983. In that role, she supplements services offered by attorneys in independent adoption, and teaches classes on adoption. Ms. Kaplan has worked professionally in the world of adoption since 1964, in both public and private agencies. She has spent the better part of her career placing special-needs children. Ms. Kaplan is a Fellow of the North America Center on Adoptions and Chairperson of the Southern Division of the California Adoption Agency Association. She is a co-founder of the Orange County Adoption Council and the Open Door Society in Orange County. Ms. Kaplan has served on the boards of Court Appointed Special Advocates and the Triadoption Library and Post Adoption Center for Education and Research. She was voted Child Advocate of the Year in 1987 by the Orange County Child Abuse Council. Ms. Kaplan lectures nationally and is co-author of the *Cooperative Adoption* 1985, Triadoption Publications. She is herself an adoptive parent of special-needs children.

Ron Kral, M.S., University of Wisconsin-Milwaukee, is Coordinator of the Adoptive Family Program at the Brief Family Therapy Center in Milwaukee, Wisconsin. As a family therapist and practicing school psychologist, he has been professionally involved in issues concerning parenting, children and adoption for over 11 years. His publications include a monthly column in an adoptive parent group newsletter; two chapters with Judith Schaffer on "Adoptive Families" and "Treating Adoptive Families" in *Varient Family Forms* Sage, 1988; a book co-edited with Steve de Shazer, *Indirect Approaches in Therapy* and several pieces on the application of Brief Therapy in the school setting. Mr. Kral is a Clinical Member of the American Association for Marriage and Family Therapy.

Joan McNamara, M.S., is Associate Director of Family Resources, an adoption agency in Ossining, N.Y. She was Project Director for S.A.F.E. (Sexual Abuse Family Education), the first sexual abuse treatment and prevention program specific to adoption. Before her work with Family Resources, Ms. McNamara was a founding member and Communications Director for the North American Council on Adoptable Children, served on its Board of Directors, and chaired its committee, "Handicapped Children Are Adoptable". She was also Editor of the U.S.-Canadian publication *Adoptable*. She has lectured and presented workshops and training nationwide and in Canada. Ms. McNamara has been consultant to national media, including the Children's Television Network, and state and federal adoption projects, conferences, and programs. Ms. McNamara is the author of numerous books and articles, including *The Adoption Advisor* (1975) and *SAFE Kids*; a weekly newspaper column; and a federal government publication, *Adopting the Child With Special Needs*. She has thirteen children, of which eleven are adopted, special-needs children.

Judith Schaffer, M.A., is Co-founder and the Director of Research, the Center for Adoptive Families in New York City, New York. Ms. Schaffer has been working in the field of adoption for several years, and is the adoptive parent of two children. Along with her associates Dr. Christina Lindstrom and Mr. Ron Kral, Ms. Schaffer has authored articles and given presentations nationally on her brief family therapy and research with adoptive families.

Deborah N. Silverstein, A.C.S.W., M.S.W., University of Southern California, is a licensed clinical social worker affiliated with Parenting Resources in Tustin, California. An adoptive parent of four special-needs youngsters, she became an advocate for foster and adoptive children in Pennsylvania and California. Subsequently, she spent four years with Jewish Family Service in Orange County before joining Parenting Resources full-time. She works with all members of the adoption triad, offering education, support, and psychotherapy. She runs both in-patient and out-patient groups for adolescent adoptees. In addition, she travels around the country, often with Sharon Kaplan, offering specialized adoption training. Ms. Silverstein and Ms. Kaplan are the authors of "The Seven Core Issues in Adoption," a theoretical framework for understanding the lifelong impact of the adoption experience.

Kenneth W. Watson. M.S.S.S., Boston University, is the assistant director of the Chicago Child Care Society in Illinois, and has worked over thirty years in the field of adoption. He is currently the chairman of the Adoption Task Force of the Child Welfare League of America. Mr. Watson has served as a part-time faculty member of the Jane Addams College of Social Work at the University of Illinois at Chicago, the Professional Development Program of the School of Social Services Administration at the University of Chicago, the National Child Welfare Leadership Center of the School of Social Work at the University of North Carolina, and the Summer Institute Program of the School of Social Work at Virginia Commonwealth University.

References

Adoption Disruptions. (1981) U.S. Department of Health and Human Services. DHHS Publication #(OHDS) 81-30319, June.

Aguilera, D. C. & Messick, J. M. (1974). *Crisis Intervention: Theory and Methodology.* C.V. Mosby Company, St. Louis, MO. (p. 4).

Anderson, Carole J. (1987) *Thoughts to Consider For Newly Searching Adoptees.* Concerned United Birthparents. Des Moines, Iowa.

Arms, Suzanne. (1983) *To Love and Let Go.* New York: Alfred Knopf.

Askin, Jayne. (1982) *Search: A Handbook for Adoptees and Birthparents.* Harper and Row.

Auth, Patricia J. (1986) The Search in Adoption: A Service and A Process, *Social Casework,* Vol 67(9), November.

Auth, Patricia J. and Shirley Zaret. (1986) The Search in Adoption: A Service and a Process, *Social Casework,* November, 560-568.

Baran, Annete, Reuben Pannor and Arthur Sorosky. (1984) Open Adoption as Standard Practice, *Child Welfare,* Vol. LXIII #3, May/June.

Barth, Richard P., Marianne Berry, Mary Lou Carson, Regina Goodfield, Barry Feinberg. (1986) Contributors to Disruption of Older-Child Adoptions, *Child Welfare,* Vol, LXV(4), July/August.

Beckstead, Gayle and Mary Lou Kozub (1984) *Searching In Illinois,* ISC Publications, Costa Mesa, CA.

Berman, Lauren and Rhea K. Bufferd. (1986) Family treatment to address loss in adoptive families. *Social Casework,* January 3-11.

Blotcky, Mark J., John G. Looney, and Keith D. Grace. (1982) Treatment of the Adopted Adolescent: Involvement of the Biologic Mother, *Journal of the American Academy of Child Psychiatry*, Vol, 21(3), May 281-285.

Bohman, M. & Sigvardsson, S. (1982). Adoption and fostering as preventive measures. In E. J. Anthon & C. Chiland (Eds.) *The Child in His Family, 7*. NY, Wiley.

Bowlby, J. (1969 - 1980), *Attachment, Separation and Loss (3 Volumes)*. NY, Basic Books.

Braden, Josephine A. (1981) Adopting the Abused Child: Live Is Not Enough, *Social Casework*, pp. 362-367.

Brockhaus and Brockhaus. (1982) Foster Care, Adoption and the Grief Process, *Journal of Psychosocial Nurse and Mental Health Services*, Vol. 20(9), September.

Brinich, P. M. & Brinich, E. B. (1982). Adoption and adaptation. *The Journal of Nervous and mental Disease* 170,(8), 489-493.

Brodzinsky, Anne. (1986) *The Mulberry Bird*, Prespective Press.

Brodzinsky, D. M. (1987) Adjustment to Adoption: A Psychosocial Perspective. *Clinical Psychology Review, 7*.

Brodzinsky, D.M., Schechter, M. E., Braff, A. M. & Singer L. M. (1984). Psychological and academic adjustment in adopted children. *Journal of Consulting and Clinical Psychology* 52, 582-590.

Brodzinsky, David, Leslie M. Singer, and Anne Braff. (1984) Children's understanding of adoption. *Child Development*.

Bunin, Sherry and Catherine. (1979) *Is That Your Sister?* Patheon.

Buntman, Peter and Eleanor Saris. (1979) *How To Live With Your Teenager: A Survivor's Handbook for Parents*. Birch Tree Press, 315 S. San Gabriel Blvd., Pasadena, CA 91107.

Bush, Malcolm and Harold Goldman. (1982) Psychological Parenting and Permanency Principles in Child Welfare: A Reappraisal and Critique, *American Journal of Orthopsychiatry*, Vol, 52(2), April

Cain, W. C. (1980). *Theories of Development*. Englewood Cliffs, NJ, Prentice Hall, Inc.

Campbell, Lee. (1979) *Understanding the Birthparent*. Concerned United Birthparents. Des Moines, Iowa (1987 reprint).

Carney, Ann. (1976) *No More Here and There—Adopting the Older Child*. North Carolina University Press.

Chiaradonna, William. (1982) A Group Work Approach to Post-Surrender Treatment of Unwed Mothers, *Social Work With Groups*, Vol. 5(4).

Children's Home Society of Minnesota (1984). *Model Statement on Post-Legal Adoption Services*. St. Paul, MN.

Cohen, Joyce. (1981) *Adoption Breakdown With Older Children*. Unversity of Toronto, Faculty of Social Work, Monograph Series.

Coleman, Loren (1987) *Suicide Clusters*, Boston and London, Faber and Faber, Inc.

Cordell, Antoinette S., Cicely Nathan and Virginia P. Krymov. (1985) Group Counseling for Children Adopted at Older Ages, *Child Welfare*, Vol. LXIV. #2, March/April 113-123.

Coyne, A. (1983). Bonding and attachment, *Adoptalk*, July/August.

De Shazer, S. (1982). *Patterns of Brief Family Therapy*. NY, Guilford.

De Shazer, S. (1985). *Keys to Solutions in Brief Therapy*. NY, W.W. Norton.

De Shazer, S. and Molnar, A. (1984). Four useful interventions in brief family therapy, *The Journal of Marital and Family Therapy* 10, 297-304.

De Shazer, S., Berg, I. K., Lipchik, E., Nunnally, E., Molnar, A., Gingerich, W., & Weiner-Davis, M. (1986). Brief therapy: Focused solution development. *Family Process* 25, 207-221.

Deutsch, Swanson, Bruell, Cantwell, Weinberg, and Baren. (1982) Overrepresentation of Adoptees in Children with the Attention Deficit Disorder, *Behavior Genetics*, Vol. 12, #2, March.

Edwards, J., Ruskin, N. & Turrini, P. (1981). *Separation-Individuation: Theory and Application*. NY, Gardner Press, Inc.

Elkind, D. (1979). *The Child and Society*. NY, Oxford Press.

Erickson, E. H. (1963). *Childhood and Society*. (2nd ed.) NY, W. W. Norton and Company, Inc.

Fahlberg, Vera. (1981) *The Child in Placement: Common Behavioral Problems*. Michigan Department of Social Services.

Fahlberg, Vera. (1979a) *Attachment and Separation*. Michigan Department of Social Services.

Fahlberg, Vera. (1979b) *Helping Children When They Must Move*. Michigan Department of Social Sevices.

Fales, M. J. (1985). *Post-Legal Adoption Services Today*. NY, Child Welfare League of America.

Feigelman, W. & Silverman, A. R. (1979). Preferential adoption; A new mode of family formation, *The Journal of Contemporary Social Work* 60, 296-305.

Feigelman, W. & Silverman, A. (1983). *Chosen Children, New Patterns of Adoptive Relationships*. NY; Praeger Publishers.

Festinger, Trudy. (1986) *Necessary Risk: A Study of Adoptions and Disrupted Adoptive Placements*. Child Welfare League of America.

Flavell, J. H. (1963 edition). *The Developmental Psychology of Jean Piaget*. D. Vann Nostrand Company.

Frank, Jack with Laurie Flynn. (1983) Group Therapy for Adopted Adolescents and Their Families, *Child Today*, March/April.

Gesell, Ilg, Ames, et al. (n.d), *The First Five Years of Life*. Gesell Institute of Child Development.

Gill, Margaret (1978) "Adoption of Older Children: The Problems Faced." *Social Casework*, 59(3), pp. 272-278.

Gilman, Lois. (1984) *The Adoption Resource Book*.

Golan, N. (1978). *Treatment in Crisis Situations*. The Free Press, pp. 48, 49.

Grabe, P., ed. (1986). *Adoption Resources for Mental Health Professionals*. Mercer, PA; Children's Aid Society in Mercer County.

Hallen Beck, Carol A. (1984) *Our Child: Preparation for Parenting in Adoption.* Our Child Press, Wayne, Pennsylvania.

Hartman, Ann. (1978) Diagrammatic Assessment of Family Relationships. *Social Casework*, 59(8) (October).

Hartman, Ann. (1984) *Working with Adoptive Families Beyond Placement.* N.Y. Child Welfare League of America.

Hartman, Ann (1979) *Finding Families: An Ecological Approach to Family Assessment in Adoption.* Volume 7. Beverly Hills: Sage.

Hess, Peg. (1982) Parent-Child Attachment Concept: Crucial for Permacy Planning, *Social Casework*, January.

Hoopes, Janet L. (1982) *Prediction in Child Development, A Longitudinal Study of Adoptive and Nonadoptive Families The Delaware Family Study.* Child Welfare League of America.

Hooper, Janet L. (1985) *Identity Formation in Adopted Adolescents,* Child Welfare League of America.

Jewett, Claudia L. (1978) *Adopting the Older Child.* The Harvard Common Press. Harvard, MA.

Jewett, Claudia L. (1982) *Helping Children Cope with Separation and Loss.* The Harvard Common Press. Harvard, MA.

Johnston, Patricia Irwin. (1984) *The Adoptor's Advocate.* Prespectives Press.

Johnston, Patricia Irwin, editor. (1983) *Perspectives on a Grafted Tree.* Prespective Press.

Kaplan, Sharon and Mary Jo Rillera. (1984) *Cooperative Adoption.* Triadoption Library Press.

Kantor, Deborah. *Adoption and Abandonment: A Somatic Psychotherapeutic Perspective.* Ph.D. Disseration (2431 Second Street, Santa Monica, CA 90405).

Katz, Linda. (1980) Adoption Counseling as a Preventive Mental Health Specialty, *Child Welfare*, LIX, March 161-162.

Katz, Linda. (1986) Parental Stress and Factors for Success in Older Child Adoptions, *Child Welfare*, Vol. LXV(6), November/December.

Kinney, J., Haapala D., Booth, C & Assoc. (1977) *Overview of the Homebuilder Program.* Behavioral Sciences Institute, 1717 A. 341st Place, Federal Way, WA 98003.

Kinney, J., Haapala D. & Gast, J. E. (1987). Assessment of families in crisis, from Bryce, M. & Hoyd, J. (Eds.) *Treating Families in the Home: An Alternate to Placement.* Springfield, IL., Charles C. Thomas.

Kirk, H. D. (1981). *Adoptive Kinships.* Port Angeles, WA, Ben-Simon Publications.

Kirk, David. (1964) *Shared Fate.* New York: Free Press.

Kirk, H. D. (1984). *Shared Fate: A Theory and Method of Adoptive Relationships.* NY, Free Press 1964. (revised edition) Port Angeles, WA; Ben-Simon Publications.

Klibanoff, Susan and Elton (1973). *Let's Talk About Adoption.* Little, Brown & Co., Boston.

Knight, Mary R. (1985) Termination Visits in Closed Adoptions, *Child Welfare,* Vol. LXIV(1), January/February.

Kohlberg, L. (1978). The Cognitive Developmental Approach to Behavior Disorder: A Study of the Development of Moral Reasoning in Delinquents. *Cognitive Defects in the Development of Mental Illness.* Serlan, G.(ed.). Brunner, M.

Kowal, Katherine A. and Karen Maitland Schilling. (1985) Adoption Through the Eyes of Adult Adoptees, *Journal of American Orthopsychiatry.*

Kraft, Adrienne D. et al. (1985) Some Theoretical Considerations on Confidential Adoptions, Part I: The Birth Mother, Part II: The Adoptive Parent, Part III: The Adopted Child, Part IV: Countertransference, *Child and Adolescent Social Work.*

Kral, R. & Schaffer, J. (1988). Treating the adoptive family. In *Families in Trouble: Families With Problems Related to Alternate Life Styles, 5,* (Ed.) Chilman, C., Cox, F., & Nunnally, E. Sage Press (in press). Chapter 10.

Kral, R., Schaffer, J. & De Shazer, S. (1987). Adoptive Families: More of the same and different. (Unpublished manuscript).

Krementz, Jill. (1983) *How It Feels To Be Adopted.* New York: Alfred Knopf.

Kubler-Ross, E. (1969). *On Death and Dying.* NY, Macmillan Publishing Co.

Lander, Joyce (1977) *Mixed Families: Adopting Across Racial Boundaries.* Doubleday.

LePere, Dorothy W. , Lloyd E. Davis, Janus Couve, and Mona McDonald. (1986) *Large Sibling Groups Adoption Experiences.* Child Welfare League of America.

Lifton, B. J. (1979). *Lost and Found: The Adoption Experience.* NY, Dial Press.

Lifton, Betty Jean. (1975) *Twice Born.* McGraw Hill.

Lifton, Betty Jean. (1981) *I'm Still Me.* Alfred Knopf.

Lindsay, Jeanne Warren. (1979) *Pregnant Too Soon.* Morning Glory Press.

Lindsay, Jeanne Warren. (1986) *Open Adoption: A Caring Option.* Morning Glory Press.

Livingston, Carole. (1978) *Why Was I Adopted?* Lyle Stuart.

Mackie, Alastair J. (1982) Families of Adopted Adolescents, *Journal of Adolescence,* 5:167 - 179

Mahler, M., Pine, F. & Bergman, A. (1975). *The Psychological Birth of the Human Infant.* NY, Basic Books.

Martin, Cynthia. (1979) *Beating the Adoption Game.* La Jolla, CA.: Oaktree Publishers.

Mason, Mary Martin, ed. (1987) *The Mircale Seekers: An Anthology of Infertility.* Prespectives Press.

McNamara, Joan. (1975) *The Adoption Adviser.* New York: Hawthorn Books.

McRoy, Zurcher, Lauderdale, Anderson. (1982) Self-esteem and Racial Identity in Transracial and Inracial Adoptees, *Social Casework,* November.

Mech, Edmund V. (1986) Pregnant Adolescents: Communicating the Adoption Option. *Child Welfare, V*ol. LXV(6), November/December.

Melina, Lois Ruskai. (1986) *Raising Adopted Children: A Manual for Adoptive Parents.* NY, Harper and Row.

Melina, L. R. (1975). *Raising Adopted Children: A Manual For Adoptive Parents.* NY, Harper and Row.

Menning, Barbara Eck. (1977) *Infertility: A Guide for the Childless Couple.* Prentice Hall.

Millen, Leverett and Samuel Roll. (1985) Solomon's Mothers: A Special Case of Pathological Bereavement, *Journal of American Orthopsychiatry.*

Musser, Sandra K. (1979) *I Would Have Searched Forever.* Jan Enterprises.

Nelson, K. A. (1985). *On the frontier of adoption: A study of special-needs adoptive families.* NY, Child Welfare League.

Nerlove, Evelyn. (1985) *Who Is David?* Child Welfare League of America.

Pannor, Reuben and Evelyn Nerlove. (1977) Fostering Understanding Between Adolescents and Adoptive Parents Through Group Experiences, *Child Welfare,* Vol. LVI, #8, September/October.

Patridge, Susan; Hornby, Helaine; and McDonald, Thomas (1986) *Learning From Adoption Disruption: Insights for Practice,* Portland, Maine, University of Southern Maine.

Perlmutter, J. (1972). A model for Griefwork, Unpublished lectures presented at George Williams College; Summer Institute, Group Dynamics.

Plumez, Jacqueline Horner. (1982) *Successful Adoption.* Harmony Books.

Poole, Lyman, McBoog, Barbee, Martin and Dechant. (1984) Adoption: The Family Physician's Role, *The Journal of Family Practice,* Vol 19, #4, 1984.

Powell, John Y. (1985) *Whose Child Am I? Adults' Recollections of Being Adopted.* Tiresias Press.

Powers, Douglas, Editor. (1984) *Adotpion for Troubled Children Prevention and Repair of Adoptive Families Through Residential Treatment.* New York: Haworth Press.

Powledge, Fred. (1982) *So You're Adopted.* Charles Scribner's Sons.

Reid, William J. Richard McKagen, Alison Kaminsky, and
Katherine Helmer. (1987) Adoptions of Older Institutionized
Youth, *Social Casework*, March 140 -149.

Rickarby, G.A. and Pauline Egan. (1980) Issues of Preventive
Work With Adopted Adolescents, *Medical Journal of
Australia*, pp. 470-472, May 17.

Rillera, Mary Jo. (1981) *The Adoption Searchbook*. Triadoption
Publications.

Sanders, Pat and Nancy Sitterly. (1981) *Search Aftermath and
Adjustments*. ISC Publications.

Schaffer, J. & Kral, R. (1988). Adoptive Families. *In Families in
Trouble: Families with Problems Related to Alternate Life Styles,
5*. (Ed.) Chilman, C., Cox, F., & Nunnally, E. Sage Press (in
press). Chapter 9.

Segal, Robert M., (1984) Helping Children Express Grief
Through Symbolic Communication, *Social Casework*,
December 590 - 598.

Shapiro, Constance Hoenk and Betsy Crane Seeber. (1983) Sex
Education and Adoptive Family, *Social Casework*, pp. 291-
296, July / August.

Shaw, Martin. (1983) Looking Back: Natural Parents, *Adotpion
and Fostering*, Vol. 7(3).

Sherman, Sheldon. (1982) *How To Get Pregnant*. Scribner
Publishing Company.

Sherwin, Laurie and Dorothy Smith. (1983) *Mothers and Their
Adopted Children: A Bonding Process*. New York: Tiresias
Press, Inc.

Silber, Kathleen and Phyllis Speedlin. (1983) *Dear Birthmother:
Thank You For Our Baby*. Corona Publishing Company.

Silverman, Phyllis R. (1981) *Helping Women Cope With Grief*. Sage
Publications.

Silverstein, Deborah N. and Sharon Kaplan. (1982) Theory of
"core issues" in adoptive development. Unpublished mss.

Silverstein, Deborah N. (1985) Identity Issues in the Jewish
Adopted Adolescent, *Journal of Jewish Communal Service*.
Summer.

Simos, B. G. (1979). *A Time to Grieve: Loss as a Universal Human Experience.* NY, Family Service Association of America.

Singer, L. M., et al. (1985, December). Mother infant attachment in adoptive families, *Child Development, 56.*

Smith, D. & Sherwen, L. (1983). *Mothers and Their Adopted Children: The Bonding Process.* NY, Tiresias Press.

Smith, Jerome. (1981) *You're Our Child: A Social/Psychological Approach to Adoption.* University Press of America.

Sommer, Susan. (1984) *And I'm Stuck With Joseph.* Herald Press, (165 Pittsburgh, Scottsdale, Pa 15683-1798).

Sorosky, A., Baran, A., & Pannor, R. (1978). *The Adoption Triangle: The Effects of the Sealed Record on Adoptees, Birth Parents and Adoptive Parents.* Garden City, NY, Anchor Press/Doubleday.

Sorosky, Arthur D. et al. (1975) Identity Conflicts in Adoptees, American, *Journal of Orthopschiatry,* 45 (1), pp. 18-27, January.

Stein, Sara Bonnett. (1979) *The Adopted One.* New York: Walher and Co.

Tienari, P. Sorri, A., Lahti, I., Naarala, M., Wahlberg, K.E., Ronkko, T., Moring, J. & Pohjola J. (1978). Family environment and the etiology of schizophrenia; Implications from the Finnish adoptive family study of schizophrenia, in *Familiar Realities: The Heidelberg Conference.* (Eds.) H. Stierlin, F.B. Simon and Gunther Schmidt, NY, Brunner/Mazel.

Tilbor, Karen; Coleman, Loren; Porter, Dan; and Hudson, Ella (1987) *Adoption-A Lifelong Process* (video), University of Southern Maine/Expanded Video, Inc., Portland, Maine.

Triseliotes, John (1980) *In Search of Origins: The Experience of Adopted People,* Routledge & Kegan Paul, Boston.

Ward, Margaret. (1984) Sibling Ties in Foster Care and Adoption Planning, *Child Welfare,* Vol. LXIII, #4, July/August.

Wheeler, Candace. (1978) *Shared Adventure.* Winking Owl Press, (P.O. Box 104039, Anchorage, Alaska, 99510).

Wheeler, Candace, (1978) *Where Am I Going?* Winking Owl Press.

Wilkinson, Hei Sook Park. (1985) *Birth Is More Than Once.*

Winkler, Robin and Van Keppel. (1984) *Relinquishing Mothers in Adoption: Their Lifelong Adjustment.* Melbourne: Institute of Family Studies.

Zwimpfer, Diane M. (1983) Indicators of Adoption Breakdown, *Social Casework.* March.